STRATFORD-UPON-AVON
BLUE
MOTOR SERVICES
Remembered

David Harvey

Frontispiece: A Stratford Blue bus in Stratford-Upon-Avon.

ALLAN T. CONDIE PUBLICATIONS

Above: Midland Red took over ownership of the Leamington & Warwick bus fleet after 30th September 1937. Only two of their 12 Daimler CF6 buses were operated by Stratford Blue. Following withdrawal, the remaining ten buses are seen dumped in a field just over Clapton Bridge. All subsequently went for scrap. (M. Rooum Collection).

Frontispiece

The West Green Drive L2 service was a town route which took a semi-circular course to Shottery and then on to the Alcester Road end of the estate. 17, (2767 NX), a Leyland "Titan" PD3/4, with a Willowbrook body, by now, in 1970, renumbered 28, is seen in West Green Drive, an area of 1950s housing. The L2 service was one of those which terminated in Bridge Street, rather than the usual bus station. (A.T.Locke)

Contents

ISBN 1 85638 035 1 Paperback

Series Editor: Allan T. Condie

Design, layout and reproduction by Rivers Media Services.   Printed in England.

Allan T. Condie Publications

40 Main Street, Carlton, NUNEATON CV13 ORG. Tel./Fax 01455-290389

Preface

Stratford-upon-Avon Blue Motor Services provided the town of Stratford-upon-Avon and the surrounding area of south Warwickshire with regular and efficient bus services. This volume attempts to capture the 'feel' of the Company's operations, through its buses, routes and operating environment.

This volume traces the history of these companies and their growth by the use of photographs of horse trams, electric trams and motor buses of the Leamington and Warwick Electrical Company and the tiny Stratford-upon-Avon Motors fleet in the mid-1920s, through the days of ownership by the Balfour, Beatty Group, when the tram system was finally closed. The book examines the Stratford-upon Avon Blue Motor Services from the time that it became part of the B.E.T. Group after 1935. This pictorial album is intended to show Stratford Blue's buses in their working environment and shows what a exceptionally smart fleet it was throughout its many years of operation. There was a period of thirty-six years independence from 1935, as Stratford Blue, although it coming under the control of Midland Red throughout this time, pursued initially a vigorous policy of purchasing second-hand Tilling-Stevens single-deckers. In the 1930s until after the Second World War, operating conditions were difficult, especially as Stratford Blue had a lot of services for the military to operate.

After the delivery of the post-war Leyland double and single-deckers, the fleet, ably managed by Mr W.Agg, were a credit to the pride and effort of the staff. After his death 'in harness' in 1958, his successors continued the tradition of a smart, well maintained fleet of buses and this was the case until the final absorption by Midland Red on New Year's Day 1971. The final days of the Stratford Blue fleet after the 1971 take-over, show the surviving buses, denuded of their blue, white and silver livery and sporting the drab all-over red of its Smethwick-based owners.

The photographs also depict the Stratford Blue buses and coaches running on the long Stage Carriage Services to Evesham, Cheltenham, Coventry and Royal Leamington Spa as well as on the well-known 150 service to Birmingham, which although licensed to Midland Red, was part operated by the company.

For over thirty years, after the Second World War, Stratford had the River Avon, medieval buildings, William Shakespeare, his plays, his family and 'his Stratford' and the theatre and ever increasing hoards of visitors from home and abroad. At this time, the smart blue and white double-decker buses, so beloved by the American tourists, continued to ply their trade; perhaps only the red London buses were better known? Alas, it was only when they had gone that even the non-bus enthusiast realised what an asset the town had lost!

Acknowledgements

This book would have been impossible to write had it not been for that most vital and often forgotten source-the photographers. Transport photographers seem to have been around since William Fox Talbot photographed the "S.S. Great Britain" in Bristol in 1843, which was only about five years after the process of calotype negatives had been invented. The earliest photograph in this volume is confirmed as being taken in 1890, when some brave soul with a tripod and a huge wooden plate camera, on a bright, sunny summers day, took a blurred shot of a horse-tram in the Parade, Royal Leamington Spa. It is a sobering thought that the last photograph in the book was taken nearly one hundred and ten years later.

Before thanking individual photographers, the most important person to thank, however is my wife Diana, who gave me the time and opportunity to undertake the compilation of this book.

Many of the photographers, whose work is included herein, can be easily identified, but in certain cases, this has been extremely difficult. If any photographs have been incorrectly attributed, then sincere apologies are offered. I would especially like to thank Alan Cross, Alistair Douglas, Chris Heaps, David Little, Roy Marshall, Les Mason, Arnold Richardson of Photobus, Mike Rooum, who also, most generously, gave me access to some extremely rare timetables and photographs, Michael Shaw of the Oxford Bus Museum and Ray Simpson and of course all those unknown photographers who supplied the late Bob Mack with negatives to print. Alan Mills of the Omnibus Society kindly gave me access to the late John Cull's negatives, while the library staff of the National Tramway Museum at Crich allowed me to search for one particular Leamington and Warwick tram photograph in their negative collection.

Special thanks are due to the Shakespeare Guild Library in Stratford and Warwick County Library. In both cases the staff were exceedingly helpful and allowed me a free reign to access material. The D.V.L.C. in Swansea and the P.S.V. Circle must be thanked for their help in providing most of the vehicle information.

Sylvia Jones at Companies House in Cardiff was extremely helpful and supplied me with a lot of useful and informative background material.

I would also like to thank Tony Hall and Richard Weaver for their sterling work in proof reading the manuscript, to Roger Carpenter who worked wonders with some very old negatives and to Barry Ware who provided the destination blind information and was always prepared to listen. A cryptic word of thanks is due to Ian Stuart of the "Waggon & Horses" public house in Oldbury, but that is another story!

Finally a warm acknowledgement is due to Allan Condie, who approached me with an idea which grew at an alarming rate 'like Topsy', into this volume which you are about to read. His interest and knowledge about tickets and ticket machines was most valuable, while his unfailing enthusiasm for the project was a vital factor in producing a book which tells the whole story, or as near as one has been allowed to tell, of Stratford-upon-Avon Blue Motor Services.

Memories of Stratford Blue

In the days before my parents owned a car, occasionally we would "go somewhere" on a Sunday for the day by bus. As we lived in Sparkhill, that somewhere would be either Stratford or Warwick.

As a child I loved Warwick, not just because of its castle but because of its old buildings in Jury Street and High Street. The Market Place was fascinating, because although it was always a hive of activity, it was almost a secret square with hidden entrances in all the corners.

Stratford was to me less interesting and full of people 'looking at things', people who I now know were tourists. But the one thing which going to Stratford had over a trip to Warwick, was the journey by bus; if you got it right, it was a Stratford Blue vehicle. In Birmingham we had the dignified Birmingham Corporation blue and cream everywhere, which was wonderful. Midland Red painted a bleaker picture with lining-out and black wings being replaced by all-over spray-painted red. Then out of a bright blue day came a bright blue bus with white window surrounds and a silver roof, working on the 150 service, 'On Hire To Midland Red'.

One hot, thundery Sunday, it was decided that we would go to Stratford, so we walked to the St John's Road stop and waited and waited and waited. Eventually two Midland Reds came along which were an LD8 and a FEDD. Of course both were full with standing passengers hanging on to every seat frame. My dad was by now getting hot and fraught and had lit up his pipe several times by the time the thunderstorm broke. The three of us and the dog, Monty, sheltered in a doorway designed for two and we were at the point of going home, when out of the spray emerged a fairly new MAC-registered Leyland!

The old joke of the late, great Chic Murray comes to mind about "dogs must be carried", when I remember, all those years ago, struggling upstairs with Monty, into a hell-hole of dripping windows and steaming, sweaty bodies. We managed to get the back seat and the one in front of it alongside the staircase as by this time we were now speeding through Springfield on our way to Hall Green and that place just beyond Birmingham with a girl's name.

My memory of this journey, other than being very wet and having to nurse an even wetter dog on my knee, was the speed at which we travelled. We were through Shirley and Hockley Heath in what seemed like a few minutes and as we came to the top of Liveridge Hill, to drop down the escarpment of the Birmingham Plateau and into the Avon Valley, the rain stopped. By the time we went under the long since demolished railway bridge in Henley-in-Arden the sun was out and all was well with the world.

A lot of people got off in Henley that day and I left my parents and the dog and went down stairs to sit behind the driver and watch him change gear - something I would have gladly have done as I was still soaked! The smartly painted lower saloon of the Leyland bus body contrasted with the polished wood interiors of Birmingham's Leyland-bodied PD2s. Of course the clunk of the electric doors fitted to these buses was something very rarely heard in Birmingham, unless you travelled on 'The Red's' D5Bs.

Taking all this in as well as watching the proficiency of the driver and listening for the typical Leyland clutch judder as we pulled away from the stop, made me forget Wootten Wawen aqueduct. We sped past the old flour mill and suddenly there was this low iron beam-thing across the road threatening to decapitate mum and dad on the top deck! I was frozen in terror, half standing as if to warn the driver and half sitting because if we did hit the aqueduct then I was just that bit lower and might not be hit by the bridge. The Leyland didn't even slow down! The driver kept his foot hard down on the throttle and we whizzed beneath the bridge. To this day, even in a car, I still feel a cold shiver up my spine when I'm travelling along the old Stratford Road and see that canal aqueduct.

Of course we all survived. When we arrived in Stratford at the Red Lion bus station, my dad had just relit his pipe and was having a contented St Bruno moment while mum was just content at arriving. MAC seemed all in one piece and the driver was telling the conductor with the aid of some added, previously unheard-of adjectives, just how bad the weather had been coming out of Birmingham.

Me? After the threat of a grisly demise on Stratford Road, the rest of the journey was a white knuckled ride as I held on for grim death and not daring to look. I hadn't seen Bearley railway bridge, which was nearly as low as the one at Wootten Wowen and I missed what in later years became the star attraction of Stratford - Bird's bus scrapyard! Of course, I couldn't tell my parents about what had happened, but mum kept giving me very strange looks as I repeatedly and surreptitiously examined both my parents' necks.

A walk around Bancroft Gardens, a long look at the sole remaining waggon from the Moreton-in-Marsh tramway, another walk, this time along the banks of the Avon and then another perambulation into the town for a pot of tea and as I remember a very stale toasted tea-cake. All this time dad was telling me all about the different types of Elizabethan buildings and what 'jettying' was, all of which in later years was to be most interesting; however at the time....!

But on this Sunday, in I suppose 1956, I was in a state of unbridled, but heavily suppressed terror. The day out in Stratford was wrecked because at some point we had to go back home, and all the 150s were run by double-deckers. Even the prospect of a ride once again on one of those smart Stratford Blue buses could not make my inner panic go away, because we had to go back through Wootten Wowen!

Stratford Blue In Colour

Colour drawings reveal detail about vehicles that might be easily missed on a photograph. Allan T. Condie's computer drawings reveal subtle details that would otherwise go unnoticed.

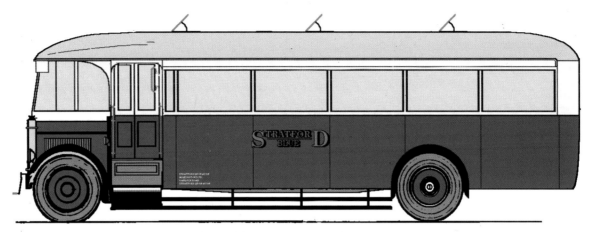

Former West Yorkshire Road Car Tilling-Stevens B10A2 of 1930.

JO 2354 - 1930 ex-City of Oxford M.S. A.E.C."Regent" with Park Royal body.

1948 - GUE - registered Leyland "Tiger" PS1 with a N.C.B. body.

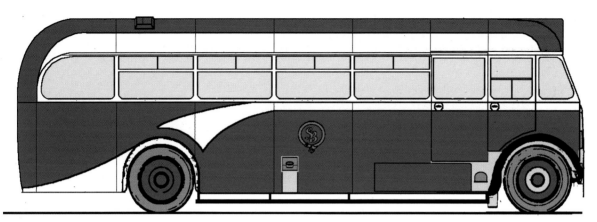

1950 - JUE-registered dual-purpose Willowbrook bodied Leyland "Tiger" PS2/3.

1948 - GUE - registered Leyland-bodied Leyland "Titan" PD2/1.

1952 - One of the 27 foot long "Farington"-style Leyland "Titan" PD2/12s.

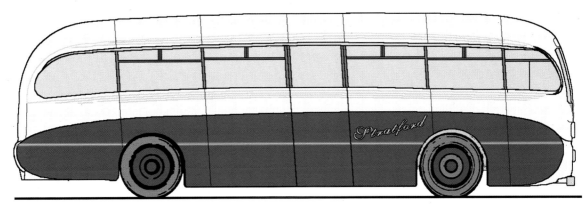

1954 - One of the pair of Burlingham "Seagull"-bodied Leyland "Royal Tigers".

1956 - A TNX-registered Willowbrook-bodied Leyland "Titan" PD2/12.

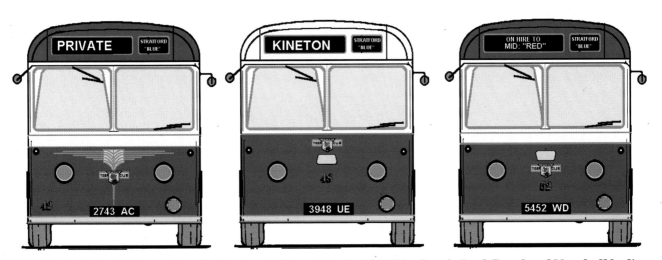

1959/1960/1962 - B.E.T.-style bodied Leyland "Tiger Cubs" with Willowbrook, Park Royal and Marshall bodies.

1963 - A Northern Counties double-deck rebody on a Leyland "Tiger" PS2/3 chassis.

1964 - HNX -registered Leyland "Titan" PD3A/1 with a Willowbrook body.

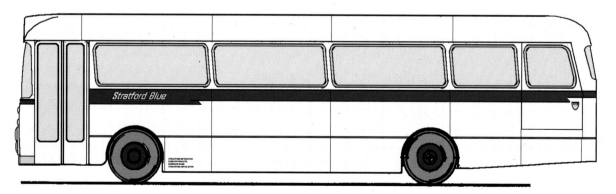

1970 - The Last One. The ubiquitous Alexander 'Y'-type body, unique to Stratford Blue.

The STRATFORD Story
BLUE

Introduction

In 1995, Stratford-upon-Avon attracted no less than 2.3 million people, who spent £99 million to enjoy the hands-on experiences of Shakespeare's home town. Stratford's half-timbered buildings in High Street and Sheep Street have all the 'Olde Worlde' charm which travellers from abroad, who number 28% of all visitors, seem to crave. During the summer months, the town is awash with camera carrying, souvenir-collecting tourists who are also on the Shakespeare trail. William Shakespeare, the Bard of Stratford, was born and died in the town and much of the town's tourist trade is devoted to the exploitation of his connections with Stratford. The architectural value of these links, such as the Birth Place, Ann Hathaway's cottage at Shottery and New Place, his last home in Stratford, is minor, but they are extremely well presented and act as magnets for hundreds of coach loads of tourists in the summer season. The Royal Shakespeare Theatre, opened in 1932, on a site alongside the Avon, is the focus for thespian activity in the town, and traditionally regarded as the authoritative centre for the productions of Shakespeare's plays, when quite often they are not!

Yet the charm of Stratford is to be able to strip away this veneer of souvenir shops, open-top bus rides and thespian activities, to reveal a delightful, thriving Elizabethan market town. Standing at an important river crossing, which was extensively redeveloped in the Georgian period, it grew as an important town on the railway route south from Birmingham and which has, since the opening of the nearby M40 motorway, become an important commuter settlement for the West Midlands Conurbation.

Stratford owes its position to the River Avon. In prehistoric times the alluvial river gravels were ideal for Neolithic and Bronze age settlement and travel. The Romans were aware of the advantages of the area and two of their roads, the Saltway from the Roman town at Alcester and the Fosse Way, crossed at the fording point on the site of present day Stratford. The first record of the name 'Stratford' occurs in A.D.691 when the local monastery of 'Stretford' (Anglo-Saxon for 'Street Ford' - a road with a river crossing) is referred to. By the time of the Domesday Book, the settlement had reached 150 souls and in 1195 the towns' Market Charter was given. Within seventy years Stratford could boast three corn mills and a fulling mill, while in 1482, Clopton Bridge, the main crossing point of the River Avon in the town was constructed. This enabled the town to resume its importance as a routeway centre and as a result began to thrive. By the time of William Shakespeare, the town was described as "a proper little market town" (Camden). A series of fires in the early part of the seventeenth century seriously damaged Stratford and it is for this reason that so much Georgian development took place in the town. This new building and the subsequent growth of the town in the eighteenth century was in part a result of the development of new modes of transport into the town.

Early Transport Developments In Stratford

The River Avon had for many years been seen as an obstacle to be crossed rather than a resource to be used as a method of transport until resourceful and far-sighted engineers made the river navigable to shallow draught vessels in 1638. The development of the Avon Navigation meant that small shipping could reach Stratford from the River Severn at Tewkesbury. This further enhanced the market prospects in the town. Although the actor David Garrick described Stratford as "the most dirty, unseemly, ill-paved, wretched-looking town in all Britain", (much worse was said about Birmingham and more often!), by 1769 David Garrick was appearing in the first Shakespeare Festival and Stratford was getting its first taste of the tourist trade! By 1817, twenty-four coaches a day were calling at Stratford. The previous year, 1816, after twenty-three years construction, the Stratford Canal was opened. This linked the Worcester Canal at Kings Norton, some 25 1/2 miles, 56 locks and one tunnel away with the Avon Navigation and further enhanced the town's position as a transport junction. The final act of the canal and turnpike age in the Stratford area was the opening of the 16 mile long Stratford & Moreton Tramway, for the 'carriage of coal, corn, timber and all other minerals' on Tuesday 5 September 1826.

This horse-drawn tramway started at the canal basin alongside the River Avon and was instrumental in making access to Moreton-in-Marsh and South Warwickshire easier. The tramway, however was not the financial success that its proposers had hoped. It worked fairly successfully as an operational enterprise until the early 1840s when the threat from the railways became a reality. The Oxford, Worcester & Wolverhampton Railway Company was promoted by Black Country coal owners and industrialists such as Lord Dudley and had the backing of the Great Western Railway. The line received Royal Assent on 4 August 1845 despite considerable opposition from other railway companies. With I.K.Brunel as its engineer, work started on the 89 mile Broad Gauge line exactly one year after gaining Parliamentary authorisation, but economic and political factors meant that by 1848 the work on the OW & W had ceased. The Stratford & Moreton Tramway was rented by the otherwise unborn OW & W since 1847 and they had also bought a controlling interest in the Stratford Canal! When the Oxford, Worcester & Wolverhampton Railway finally opened its mainline from Evesham to Wolvercote Junction, the horse-drawn tramway operated two daily connecting trains to Moreton-in-Marsh.

Passenger services continued until about the time the OW & W opened its 91/4 mile Honeybourne to Stratford branch line; this occurred on 12 July 1859 and effectively made the horse drawn tramway, which had been losing about £1,600 a year, redundant. The Oxford, Worcester and Wolverhampton Railway had in the same year joined forces with the Newport, Abergavenny & Hereford Railway and had reformed to become the West Midlands Railway on 1 July 1860. By 1863, this short-lived company had agreed to be taken over by the Great Western Railway with whom it had, throughout its separate existence, something of a love-hate relationship.

If the horse tramway and the canal were doomed, Stratford had gained two railway lines, the OW & W broad gauge line to the terminus in Sanctuary Street and the Great Western-worked Stratford-upon-Avon mixed-gauge line to Birmingham Road which had been opened on 10 October 1860 and gave access to the mainline from Birmingham via a branch at Hatton. A new station, the present one, was opened on 1 January 1863 and the railway situation was at last stabilised. In 1871, the East & West Junction Railway made a connection from the L.N.W.R. mainline at Blisworth to Kineton and had opened its Stratford station in 1879. At the same time, seeing a potentially lucrative short-cut cross-country route, the line was extended from Stratford to Broome Junction via what was described at the time as "a tortuous route" to Birmingham. This railway became the Stratford & Midland Junction Railway and was eventually absorbed by the Midland Railway.

The last railway development to affect Stratford was the opening of the Great Western Railway's North Warwickshire line in December 1907. This ran from Tyseley in the south-eastern suburbs of Birmingham to Bearley Junction where it joined the line to Stratford. This gave the G.W.R. both access to the increasing passenger traffic going to and from Birmingham and via the Honeybourne line, an alternative route to Cheltenham and Bristol. The town of Stratford was well and truly on the railway map and the late Victorian growth of the town is mainly attributable to the vastly improved access. Finally, the Stratford and Moreton Tramway finally saw it's last waggon movements around the canal basin during the First World War, though much of the line to Moreton had been closed years before.

But what of public transport by road?

Early Public Road Transport In And Around Stratford

The first regular motorbus operation into Stratford was by the Brailes, Shipston-on-Stour and Stratford-upon-Avon Steam Omnibus Company, (imagine the length of the fleet name!) who operated two single-deck Strakers, registered AB 53 and AB199, from December 1903 until about the summer of 1905. It was then that the Lyon Clark, McNeill and Company running under the fleet name of the Leamington and Warwick Motor Omnibus Company Limited began operations into Stratford. Their first two buses were registered AC 2 and 3 and were Milnes-Daimler 20/25 h.p. double-deckers. These were ordered to compete on a half-hourly service with the Leamington & Warwick Electrical Company and entered service on Monday 26 June 1905.

The old horse tramway between Leamington and Warwick, having been opened in 1882, was beginning to become time expired. The tramway had been purchased in 1899 by the British Electric Traction group who closed it down in February 1905. This was done so that it could be converted to electric operation and at the same time be re-gauged from 4' 8 1/2" to 3' 6". During the change-over period the tramway operated a temporary service of horse buses, but the enterprising Clark and McNeill operated their new-fangled buses for a fortnight before the electric trams entered service on 15 July. The new electric tram fleet consisted of six new open-toppers built by the Brush Company, (1-6) and six very similar three year old trams purchased from Taunton, (7-12). A further tram, superstitiously numbered 14, was added to the fleet in 1921, having been diverted from Cheltenham & District Light Railway Company and these thirteen trams ran the service between the two towns until its closure on 16 August 1930.

Two days after the electric trams were introduced, the Leamington & Warwick Motor Omnibus Company put into service a third Milnes-Daimler. Painted in a varnished wood livery with a red chassis, just like the earlier pair, this was a single-decker 18 h.p. model. What was significant about this bus was that it operated on a twice daily service between Kenilworth, Warwick, Barford, Wellesbourne Mountford and Stratford-upon-Avon. By the end of the year, this enterprising company had ceased trading and Leamington and Warwick were left to the tender mercies of the holly green and cream liveried electric trams and Stratford was once again "busless".

The next motor buses to appear in Stratford again came from Leamington. Three Brush double-deckers, owned by Midland Red and which had formerly operated in Birmingham, O 1287, 1289 and 1290 were hired in by the Leamington & Warwick Electrical Company to operate as feeders to the trams and to operate excursions to Stratford. These buses were bought by the Leamington & Warwick Company early in 1910 and with the addition of two other Brush vehicles, maintained the service before and after the transfer of the motor bus section to the British Automobile Traction Company on 8 November 1912. The Leamington & Warwick Electrical Company was sold to Balfour, Beatty and Company on 31 December of the same year. Their links with developments twenty years later in Stratford would have considerable bearing on the bus services in that area.

Buses Take Over

In the years after Great War, bus services in and around Stratford appear to have been worked as before from Leamington, but on April Fool's Day 1927, two local businessmen, George Henry Grail and Stanley Harold Joiner started a bus service between Stratford and Shottery using a Chevrolet LM with a fourteen seat body. Joiner and Grail had set up their bus service with the financial backing of certain eminent citizens (and brewers) of Stratford with the intention of attracting more people into the town from the outlying villages. Joiner and Grail named their new bus company "Stratford-upon-Avon Motor Services" and very soon became a thorn in the side of the Birmingham and Midland Motor Omnibus Company, (B.M.M.O., or Midland Red) and the Leamington & Warwick Electrical Company. By October 1927, Stratford-upon-Avon Motor Services had a total of seven Chevrolets of 'village' bus size proportions. They successfully applied for a licence to run a bus service between Stratford and Leamington and therefore over the tracks of the tramway company eastward from the Warwick tram terminus in High Street. The tramway companys fares were not protected, so the trams began to lose custom to the nippier small buses. The Leamington & Warwick Company retaliated by bringing in four almost new Tilling-Stevens B10Bs from the Balfour, Beatty-owned Midland General O.C. operating in the Mansfield, Langley Mill and Ilkeston areas.

From this point onwards, the battle for control of Stratford's road passengers was to be fought out between the locally-based newcomer and the well-established, but 'foreign' big bus operator. Stratford Blue Motors bought out the business of F.Martin of High Street, Cheltenham in 1930, which gave the company access to Evesham, Cheltenham and Malvern. The extra routes and presumably, the competition from the Leamington & Warwick buses meant that both an increase in the number of buses and an increase in their seating capacity was required. During the next three years, the company purchased eleven Thornycroft A1 or A2 models, all with Hall Lewis/Park Royal B20F bodies.

Meanwhile, back in Leamington, moves were afoot to abandon the 3.05 mile tram service between the Spa town and Warwick. The company, in line with Balfour, Beatty policy elsewhere, wanted to introduce trolleybuses; this was rejected locally and under the terms of the Leamington and Warwick Traction Act, (1928), the trams were to be closed down in favour of the Leamington and Warwick motor bus services.

Just when it appeared that the competition between the green buses of Leamington & Warwick and the locally based blue and white vehicles was going to take place in and around Stratford-upon-Avon, the Balfour, Beatty-owned Leamington & Warwick Company purchased Stratford-upon-Avon Motor Services. This take-over, which took place on 15 March 1929 was intended to preserve the monopoly of the L & W buses and while this seemed possible, the Stratford-based company retained its own identity.

The following year, on Monday 10 February 1930, the Leamington & Warwick Electrical Company closed the tramway for normal service but retained operating rights by operating workman's services until Saturday 16 August 1930. To replace the trams, the L & W purchased two batches of six Brush-bodied Daimler CF6s in September 1929 and January 1930 respectively.

For the Stratford services, five three year old Tilling-Stevens B10Bs, again with bodies built in Loughborough by the Brush Company were added to the fleet having been purchased from the Midland General Company, an associate company of Balfour, Beatty & Company Ltd, who were responsible for managing Stratford Blue. This was a repetition of what had occurred in February 1928 when the

Leamington & Warwick Company had borrowed four similar thirty seater buses from the same source.

On Monday 4 May 1931, the Stratford-upon-Avon Blue Motors Limited was formed replacing the previous company and severing any operation links with the Leamington and Warwick. The new company was floated with 15,000 x £1:00 shares being financed by the Midland General arm of the Balfour, Beatty Group. The original founders of Stratford - upon-Avon Motor Services, G.H.Grail and S.H.Joiner remained as directors along with Col. Sir Joseph Nall and Douglas Hayes from the Midland General Company and William McGill who was a director of Midland Electric Light & Power Company. A new general manager, Mr.W.Agg was placed in charge and he would remain in the post until his death in 1958. In order to comply with the terms of the 1930 Road Traffic Act, all the services inherited from the old Joiner and Grail company had been registered, but after the formation of Stratford Blue, a certain rationalisation was required. The result was that at the end of the same month, the service between Cheltenham and Malvern was swapped for a greater share on the Evesham to Cheltenham route.

An interesting experiment, worthy of mention although it was not in anyway connected with the new Stratford Blue company, was begun on 23 April 1932. The L.M.S.R. adapted a Karrier "Chaser" chassis, fitted with a Craven B26C body to run on rails as well as normally on the road by having rail wheels fitted inside the normal road pneumatics. The "Ro-Railer", although capable of changing from one mode of transport to the other in less than five minutes, had operated without much success on the Hemel Hempstead to Harpenden branch in 1931. It was registered for road use as UR 7924 and was tried out from the Welcombe Hotel to the former L.N.W.R. railway station and then on the railway line to Blisworth.

After reaching an agreement with Midland Red about operating arrangements in the Leamington area, which protected the services of both Stratford Blue and L & W, the next major development was the acquisition of the Stratford to Evesham services of the Reliance Bus Company of Bidford-on-Avon. Four small buses currently in service were taken over; two were Willowbrook-bodied Star VB4s which were about four years old and the other two were Guy ONDs. The Guys were immediately transferred to Cheltenham District becoming that companys number 1 and 2. This take-over took place on 6 June 1932 which was the same day that Midland Red took over the Reliance services radiating from Evesham. This was a short term situation as by the 10 September Midland Red withdrew from the Evesham to Cheltenham service in exchange for being able to pool the receipts of the Stratford to Leamington and the Stratford to Shipston-on-Stour services.

The Stratford Blue operation remained fairly stable for the next three years. The fleet received two demonstrators in 1932 and 1933. The first was, unusually, an Albion "Valiant" PV70 which had a Harrington bus body; it was registered WD 3338 and given the fleet number 22. The next year an A.E.C."Regal" 662, registered AMD 739 with a Harrington coach body was also demonstrated for a short time. Despite the modernity of both these

11

vehicles, neither were purchased, yet in 1933 a four year old Park Royal-bodied Commer 4PF was acquired. The need for new buses and the lack of either enthusiasm or finance from the parent Balfour, Beatty group of transport holding companies meant that new buses were not acquired by the Stratford-upon-Avon Blue Motors. For example, the next buses to come into the fleet were four ex-Cheltenham District Guy Cs with Guy B28F bodies, which were the last vehicles to be purchased before control of Stratford Blue was sold to B.M.M.O. on 30 June 1935.

Midland Red Takes Over

It was rather strange that, as events transpired, a daughter company would survive for forty-five years while the prosperous parent would succumb to the predatory 'big brother'. Midland Red's take-over of Stratford Blue meant that control had changed from the parsimonious Balfour, Beatty Group to the largest and most prosperous of the British Electric Traction, (B.E.T.). Meanwhile events elsewhere in south Warwickshire proceeded at a much faster rate. Firstly, the Leamington and Warwick Electrical Company changed its name to the Leamington and Warwick Transport Company on 30 October 1935 and within one month B.M.M.O. had acquired a controlling interest in the company. The following year, on 1 March, Midland Red bought the stage carriage services of Red House Garage Company in Coventry and acquired five locally built Maudslay ML3 buses. Three went directly to Stratford Blue but their sojourn was brief as all five were with L & W by early in 1937, while Stratford Blue again bought second-hand; this time, in August 1936, two ex-Kingfisher Service Tilling-Stevens B10A2s with Willowbrook bodies were purchased from Trent Motor Traction.

The former parent company of Leamington and Warwick Transport, still operating mainly a fleet of 1929/30 Daimler CF6s, ceased operation after 30 September 1937, when it agreed that all its services should be operated by Midland Red. Most of the seven year old green and cream buses were quickly disposed of to Stratford's own bard of the scrapyard, W.T.Bird, with the exception of UE 9323, which was purchased by Stratford Blue and ran for a further twelve months. Another of the batch was hired for a few months. The new owners of the blue buses of Stratford, instead of standardising on new 'home-made' S.O.S.-type single-deckers built in Edgbaston by Midland Red, seemed, like the previous owners, to be reluctant to invest in new buses!

The first 'new' buses bought by the B.M.M.O.-controlled company were eighteen 1928 vintage former North Western Road Car Tilling-Stevens B10A2s, registered with a variety of DB 51xx registrations. They were purchased in October 1936 and were two years older than the by now scrapped ex-L & W Daimlers CF6s. The 'new' buses had either Brush or Tilling rear-entrance bodies and were destined to be all withdrawn by the outbreak of the Second World War. It was a strange policy, that would be perpetuated for the next ten years and another twenty-four, increasingly ancient, buses!

The main event in Stratford-upon-Avon Blue Motors life occurred on New Years Day 1937, when the operation of the Kineton Green Bus service,

owned by Mrs Hunt, was taken over. Kineton Green had operated eleven vehicles and at the time of the take-over the fleet contained a number of ex-Devon General Leylands. Despite this, there were no vehicles involved in the purchase. As a result of the acquisition, Stratford Blue gained a service into Banbury for the first time and a nearly new garage at Kineton which had replaced one that had been burnt down in the summer of 1934.

The ex-N.W.R.C. Tilling-Stevens B10A2s were largely taken out of service in 1939 and were replaced by sixteen identical chassis of 1930 vintage. These came from West Yorkshire Road Car Company in October 1938 and were all registered in the WX 21xx series. Six had Tilling bodies, seven had United bodies, leaving three with Roe B32F bodies. With a network of services to Evesham, Cheltenham, Warwick and Banbury, a railway service in the area that was already beginning to show signs of decline and car ownership in these basically rural areas which was still very low, it is surprising that the Stratford Blue company was so poorly financed that it had to purchase elderly vehicles in an operating area that was both large and in parts so demanding. On 26 November 1938, two coaches operated by P.Owen & Sons of Abberley, Worcestershire were purchased. These were again Maudslay ML3s but with attractive C32R bodies built in West Bromwich by W.D.Smith.

The War and After

The outbreak of war meant an enormous increase in the carriage of military personnel. Army camps at Long Marston and R.A.F. stations such as at Gaydon and Wellesbourne Mountford had to be served. There were no new vehicles acquired for this increase in wartime traffic requirements. As there were no journeys to Birmingham, (that was Midland Red territory), double-decker operation was previously considered to be unnecessary on the rural routes. However in March 1940 a second-hand double-decker was bought. It was almost official policy to purchase something as old as possible and JO 2354 was no exception. This had been G167 in the City of Oxford Motor Services fleet and was a 1931 A.E.C. "Regent" 661 with a Park Royal H24/24R body. When it became unavailable, it was necessary for Stratford Blue to hire in either a R.E.D.D.-type or a F.E.D.D.-type from Midland Red.

In 1944 Stratford Blue's only S.O.S. to operate in P.S.V. service, an 'M' was purchased; this was HA 4942 and was then fifteen years old. In 1945 a new service between Stratford and Oxford was introduced that was jointly operated with City of Oxford Motor services. Extra vehicles were required to cover this increased traffic and three coaches were hired. An S.O.S. OLR, AHA 619, converted during the war from normal to forward control, was on extended loan for three years from 1945 until 1948 while two fairly new Leyland "Tiger" TS7s with Harrington bodies were also on hire from North Western Road Car; these were repainted in Stratford Blue livery. It was from this source that the next second-hand purchases originated. Eight DB 93xx registered Tilling-Stevens B10A2 chassis dating from 1930 which had been rebodied by Eastern Counties in 1935 arrived in late 1946, but like their predecessors, but for very different reasons, they only had a short shelf-life of four years.

A Change Of Policy - New Buses At Last

In 1947 the control of the ordering of vehicles was at last put in the hands of the Stratford Blue management. This resulted in a dramatic alteration of ordering policy.

Orders were place for eighteen new Leyland buses; eight were some of the earliest "Titan" PD2/1s to be built and were fitted with Leyland highbridge bodies. The remaining ten chassis were "Tiger" PS1 chassis and were fitted with B.E.T. Federation-style B34F bodies built by Northern Coach Builders. These bodies showed a remarkable similarity to bodies built by Brush for the B.E.T. Group. All were registered in the GUE series.

The success of these modern vehicles were the death-knell for the creaking and tinkling Tilling-Stevens. In 1950, twelve buses with JUE registration letters arrived. There were four Leyland "Tiger" PS2/3 semi-coaches were delivered with Willowbrook bodies as well as two PS2/1 bus bodied single-deckers. These saw off the last of the second-hand buses, while the double-deck fleet was augmented by another six Leyland-bodied Leyland "Titan PD2/1s. This were the last 7' 6" wide double-deckers to be purchased and were intended for the main road routes between the Warwickshire towns where the new wider Construction and Use regulations would have been an advantage.

Saturday 31 May 1952 was a momentous day for the company. It was on this spring day that Stratford-upon-Avon Blue Motor Services began operation on the prestigious 150 route from the Red Lion Bus Station in Stratford to Birmingham, which terminated outside St Martins Parish Church in the bustling Bull Ring. Probably the best equipped vehicles and certainly the most handsome double-deckers ever owned by the company were operated on this service and to create an even better impression, they were new. There were three buses which were registered MAC 570-572. They were fifty-eight seat, 8' wide Leyland-bodied Leyland "Titan" PD2/12s. They had exposed radiators and were the equivalents of the about to be delivered 100 tin-fronted SHA-registered PD2/12s for Midland Red, although when first delivered the MACs had open platforms.

Additional investment by Midland Red with a further 49,000 x £1:00 shares in December 1952, enabled further development of the company. After the take-over of the Bennett of Ilmington service to Shipston-on-Stour in February 1953, the Stratford Blue company settled down to a period of steady expansion. In 1954 two Burlingham "Seagull" bodied Leyland "Royal Tiger" coaches were purchased, while in 1956 another three Leyland "Titan" PD2/12s were delivered. As Leylands had stopped building bus bodies, the order went to Willowbrook who squeezed in sixty-three seats. They were the last 27' double-deckers to enter service.

The underfloor single-decker had arrived and as it had potential advantages for One-Man-Operation, (there were very few women drivers in those days!),

it was seen by every operator as an opportunity to cut costs. In 1959 five Willowbrook-bodied Leyland "Tiger Cub" PSUC1/1s arrived, four to dual-purpose semi-coach specification. This constant-meshed gearboxed chassis became the standard single-decker for Stratford Blue for the next three years as no less than nine more were purchased, with either Park Royal or Marshall-built B.E.T.-specification bodies.

If the "Tiger Cub" was briefly the standard Stratford Blue single-decker, then the 30' long Leyland "Titan" PD3, with a seating capacity of 73, became the equivalent double-decker. In February 1960 the first of three PD3/4 synchromesh gearbox, Willowbrook-bodied vehicles was delivered to Stratford and in January 1963 another four, this time with Northern Counties bodies, arrived. It was at this time that the company realised that they had a number of redundant Leyland "Tiger" PS2 half-cabs on their stocks, which could become a useful asset if rebodied as double-deckers. Following on from the precedent made by Yorkshire Traction and Yorkshire Woollen District, Stratford Blue had four of their PS2s chassis rebuilt and rebodied by Northern Counties. These had sixty-three seater forward entrances and were very handsome looking buses, unlike the fifth vehicle the first to be rebodied which had a Roe body in a style which can only be described as looking like a top heavy greenhouse.

The last large batches of double-deckers were two lots of Leyland "Titan" PD3A/1, totalling eight in all which for the first time had concealed radiators. Both the first batch of six of 1964 and the two 1966 vehicles were bodied by Willowbrook. Finally, in a last attempt to get up to date, in December 1967 Stratford Blue received its only rear-engined double-deckers, when three Leyland "Atlantean" PDR1/1s arrived which were fitted with ungainly-looking Northern Counties bodies .

A number of unusual purchases were made by the company in the early 1960s. 58, was a Ford Thames 570E, while the first 59 was a similarly Duple-bodied Bedford SB3. The Bedford was the only coach taken into stock from the three strong coach fleet of Warwickshire County Garage of Stratford.

After that, the Leyland "Leopard" became the standard single-decker, with five coaches, one dual-purpose semi-coach and one bus being bought. The company, usually so foot-sure and confident, seemed to be strangely indecisive about the choice of body manufacturer, as these seven single-deckers had no less than five different makers bodies on them! The "Leopards" were usually in synchromesh gearbox form for both the coach and bus fleet although the last one, and indeed the last new Stratford Blue vehicle to enter service in 1970, had a semi-automatic gearbox and a handsome Alexander 'Y'-type body .

The last single-deckers to be ordered were never operated and that was probably just as well! They were five Leyland "Panther" PSUR1A.1Rs with Marshall "Camair" B41D bodies designed for standee-operation. Delivered in October 1970, they remained unlicensed until the take-over by Midland Red because of industrial relations problems. Midland Red, obviously seeing a 'pup', sold them on to Preston Corporation in July 1971. These five must hold some sort of uneviable record having had two registrations and three liveries before entering revenue service.

The take-over of Midland Red by the National Bus Company was caused by the B.E.T. Group deciding to sell its interests in road transport. This happened in March 1969 and with that take-over, the former B.E.T. bus companies lost their individuality to the corporate blandness of the NBC. Smaller operators had to go as they did not fit with the new image and Stratford-upon-Avon Blue Motors were closed down.

Stratford-upon-Avon Blue Motors Limited was finally absorbed by the parent Midland Red on 1 January 1971. Midland Red took over the operation of 49 buses and repainted them in the comparatively drab Midland Red livery. Both of the garages at Stratford and at Kineton were kept open.

All of the PD3 front-engine double-deckers were sold to the Isle of Man Road Services in 1972, while the "Atlanteans", the last 'deckers, went to City of Oxford, reversing the movement of Stratford Blue's first double-decker. Most of the "Tiger Cubs" went to Potteries Motor Traction in the late spring of 1971, leaving only the former 59, a Marshall-bodied "Leopard" to soldier on as a driver trainer and the Alexander bodied semi-coach of 1970, the former 36, to go to Midland Red North. Happily both these have survived into preservation as have an "Atlantean", a rebodied "Tiger" double-decker and several "Titan" PD3s.

Stratford-upon-Avon Blue Motors ceased trading as an operating company in 1973 with assets of £135,000. This situation continued for another four years, when the company was finally dissolved on 6 December 1977.

Today the town of Stratford bustles with locals and tourists throughout the year, the Royal Shakespeare company still plays to full-houses, although perhaps in recent years without critical acclaim, and the swans glide gracefully on the River Avon as it still flows beneath Clopton Bridge. The green and cream open-toppers of Guide Friday run tourist runs around the town, but the disappearance of the always clean and dignified, freshly-painted blue and white Stratford Blue buses was a great loss to the ambience of the town and are still sorely missed.

Balfour, Beatty And Company

The Balfour, Beatty Company took over the tramway operations of J.G.White and Company in 1909. The main activity of the company, which it is still involved in today, was that of electricity supply. Below is listed the transport operating companys in which Balfour, Beatty and Company were involved and the dates they operated.

Dartford and District Light Railways Trams 1909-1921.

Luton Corporation Trams 1909-1923.

Cavehill and Whitewell Tramways Co Trams 1909-1911.

Llandudno and Colwyn Bay Electric Railway Trams 1910-1956. Buses 1956-1961.

City of Carlisle Electric Tramways Trams 1911-1931.

Llanelly and District Electric Supply Co Trams 1911-1933. Trolleybuses 1933-1952.

Mansfield and District Light Railway Trams 1912-1932. Buses 1914-1948.

Nottingham and Derbyshire Traction Co Trams 1912-1933. Trolleybuses 1933-1953.

Wemyss and District Trams 1912-1931. Buses 1922-1930.

Leamington and Warwick Electrical Co Trams 1912-1930. Buses 1928-1935.

Cheltenham District Light Railway Co Trams 1914-1930. Buses 1923-1950.

Scottish General Omnibus Buses 1919-1930.

Falkirk and District Tramways Trams 1920-1935.

Dunfermline and District Tramways Trams 1920-1937. Buses 1924-1937.

Midland General Omnibus Co Buses 1922-1948.

Stratford-upon-Avon Blue Motors Buses 1931-1935.

LEAMINGTON & WARWICK ELECTRICAL Co. LTD

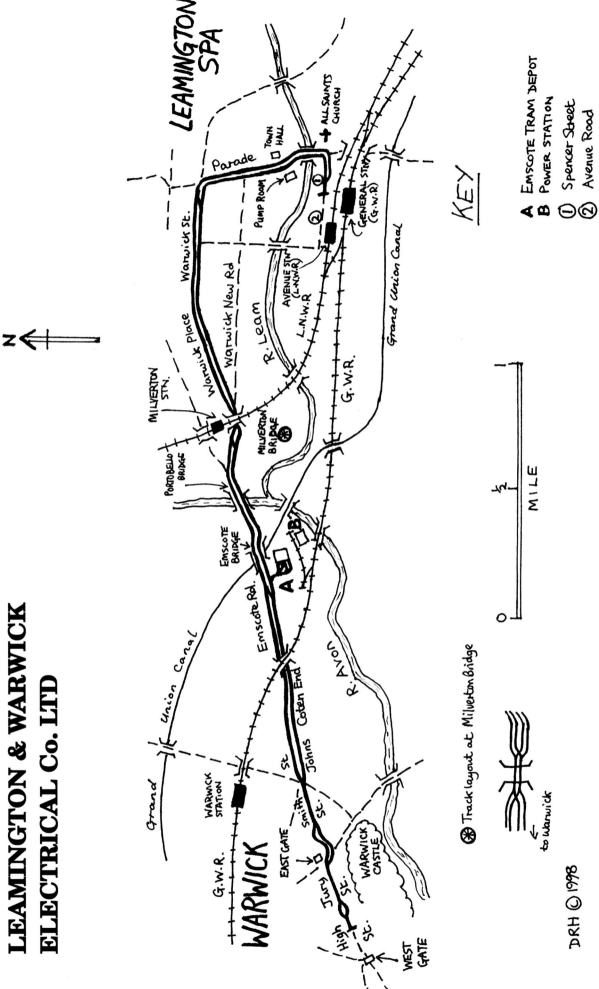

N

LEAMINGTON SPA

LEAMINGTON SPA

WARWICK

KEY

A Emscote Tram Depot
B Power Station
① Spencer Street
② Avenue Road

⊛ Track layout at Milverton Bridge

→ to Warwick

DRH © 1998

0   ½   MILE

15

Leamington And Warwick Tramways

Horse Trams

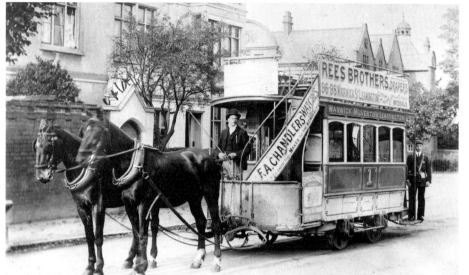

1. HORSE TRAM 1

Horse tram No.1, an open-top, forty-seater double-decker of 1881, waits near the Leamington terminus. The Leamington & Warwick Tramway system opened for passengers on 21 November 1881 and served the two towns until 15 May 1905. This five-bay tram was one of a total of nine vehicles owned by the company. This Brown, Marshall tram could be distinguished from the later ones by the curve-topped saloon windows. Notice the garden seats on the top deck. (Warwick Library)

2. HORSE TRAM 7

Standing at the Leamington terminus at the L.N.W.R. Avenue Road station is Horse Tram 7. Its crew pose proudly with their charge in the last decade of the 19th Century. The tram was built by Metropolitan Railway Carriage and Wagon Company and was one of two delivered in the Spring of 1882 which were numbered 6 and 7. The tram would move off shortly on its 34 minute journey to Warwick, just 17 yards over 3 miles away. (Warwick Library)

3. HORSE TRAM

The elevation of Leamington into Royal Leamington Spa occurred in 1838 after a visit to the 'waters' by the newly-crowned Queen Victoria. The building of the terraces on the Parade had been started in 1815 and by the early 1840s, most of the planned, grid-system, 'new-town' had been finished.

When the blurred horse tram, seen here opposite the newly completed town hall, was beginning the climb up the Parade in about 1890, many of these terraced buildings were only about fifty years old. (D. R. Harvey Collection)

Electric Trams - A journey along the route

4. CAR 1

The first of the six electric trams, No.1, an open-top, forty-eight seater built by Brush in 1905 and mounted on Brush AA trucks waits at the Avenue Road terminus when still quite new.

The tram has the B.E.T. 'wheel and magnet' crest on the side of this holly green and cream livery. The conductor with his satchel and Bell Punch ticket machine, is typically, much younger than the driver. There was a hierarchy based on age and experience, so judging by the driver, the conductor might have become a motorman about the time that the system was abandoned in August 1930! (Warwick Library)

5. CAR 8

One of the ex-Taunton and West Somerset Electric Tramways Company, Brush open-top trams, No.8 waits at the Avenue Road terminus at the stub track at the junction with Spencer Street in 1928 before setting off to Warwick. These forty-eight seaters were mounted on Brush Radial trucks which were quickly locked-up as they were prone to poor riding qualities. The ex-Taunton cars, built in 1901, were acquired by Leamington & Warwick in 1905. They were distinguishable from the 'native' trams 1 to 6 by their arch-topped saloon windows. (D.R.Harvey Collection)

6. CAR 5

In the last few years of operation, all the trams were fitted with simple three-panelled vestibuled screens. Car 5 is at the tram stop in Victoria Terrace opposite All Saints Parish Church. This impressive church was begun in 1843 and styled in an almost squashed French Gothic-style. The tram has turned out of Spencer Street from the terminus. (D.R.Harvey Collection)

7. CAR 1

On an Edwardian summers day is Leamington and Warwick's first tram, number 1. This was one of the six trams built for the Leamington & Warwick Company in 1905 by Brush of Loughborough. It is in Victoria Terrace, with the parapet of Victoria Bridge over the River Leam in the background. The bridge was completed in 1834, while Victoria Terrace itself, with its twenty-two bays, was started two years later and represents the start of the second period of the town's expansion.

The tram is about to move off into Spencer Street and to the terminus at the junction with Avenue Road at the L.N.W.R. station. (Warwick Library)

8. CAR 5

Looking from Victoria Bridge into Victoria Terrace towards the less-grand Victorian 'end of town' is Brush open-top tram 5 built in 1905. It has turned from Spencer Street on the right and has passed All Saints Church having only travelled about two hundred yards from the Leamington terminus. (Commercial Postcard)

9. CAR 8

The Regency Grace of Royal Leamington Spa's famous Pump Rooms and Public Baths, completed in 1814, stands at the bottom of the Parade at Jephson Gardens.

One of the former Taunton tramcars, 8, moves along the Parade towards the Leamington terminus. These cars were distinguishable from the trams 1-6 bought new by the company by their low-set front dash-panels.

The three soldiers on the right and the length of the women's dresses, with the emancipated lady riding the bicycle, suggest that this view was photographed immediately after the end of the Great War. (S.L. Smith Collection)

10. CAR 3

A decade earlier, Brush open-top tram, 3, travels towards the All Saints Parish Church as it passes the Pump Rooms and the Public Baths at the Jephson Gardens end of the Parade. The Gardens were first laid-out in 1834, to coincide with the opening of the Victoria Bridge and lie on both sides of the bridge. The Parade was, like much of the electric system, double-track, though here it was graced with central traction-poles with elaborately curved decorative pole-arms. (A.D. Packer Collection)

11. CAR 4

The Regency buildings on the main shopping area of the Parade in Royal Leamington Spa are among the architectural delights of the town. The Parade was laid out between 1815, the year of the Battle of Waterloo, and 1834 and were the first part of the 'planned new town'.

Tramcar 4 has come down the hill from the Warwick Street turn, in the distance, having passed a tram going up the hill towards Warwick. Car 4, still unvestibuled in this early 1920s street scene, has just left the stop opposite the Town Hall; this municipal piece of Victorian 'rhubarb', did at least create an open space at Regent Grove. The space was supervised by the omnipresent municipal statue of the late Queen. (D.R.Harvey Collection)

12. CAR 5

When Brush built tram 5 loaded up with the straw-boatered men in the Parade opposite the Town Hall, it was a warm summers Friday on 14 July 1905 and the tram was still in its first months of service. The tram was built on Brush Radial trucks but these appear to have been quickly locked-up and then substituted by AA-type trucks.

As the destination blind shows PARADE, LEAMINGTON, as the destination it suggests that the Avenue Road terminus was not used until sometime after the opening.

The massive Leamington Town Hall, built in 1883, was a large civic building that seemed totally out of place with the more subtle and delicately styled Regency buildings elsewhere in the Parade. The Regent Hotel, built in 1819, with its entrance porch supported by two large Doric columns, is a good example of the more stylish buildings of the earlier part of the century. (Commercial Postcard)

13. CAR 2

The price of Maypole Teas was 1/6d per pound when Brush-built open-top, open-vestibuled tramcar 2 of 1905 passed the provisions shop. In this Edwardian scene the tram has left the Town Hall stop in the Parade. The only other vehicular traffic is horse-drawn, ranging from four-wheeled carriages to a coal merchant's waggon on the right.

(S.L.Smith Collection)

14. CAR 12

The journey to Warwick left the Parade by way of Warwick Street. This was also part of the Regency development of Leamington. This area, on the north side of the town, was planned on a grid pattern in the 1830s ,though St Albans Church, whose tower can be seen, dates from 1877.

Ex-Taunton tram, No.5, purchased in 1905 and renumbered 12 by Leamington & Warwick, travels out of the town towards Emscote and Warwick in the first decade of the 20th century. (Commercial Postcard)

15. Warwick New Road

The large villas between Leamington and Warwick were set in walled gardens and represented all that was best in mid-nineteenth century non-industrial housing. The wide tree-lined roads inadvertently became suitable thoroughfares to carry the tram tracks, though the owners must not have been too delighted! An unidentified tram travels along Warwick Place towards the junction with Warwick New Road, as it approaches Milverton railway station bridge. (Commercial Postcard)

16. CAR 3

One of the original Leamington and Warwick electric trams, 3, stands at Milverton Station on its way to Warwick. The arch of the bridge was sufficiently low here that in order to pass beneath the centre of the arch, the track was interlaced. Needless to say, the Rules and Regulations of the Company laid down that all top-deck passengers should be seated when going underneath Milverton Bridge. The bridge was to remain a problem for many years; on 15 February 1930, a Strachan-bodied Daimler CF6 double-decker was tested underneath, but although it went through it was a fit that was too tight. Because of this the Leamington and Warwick company never operated double-deckers. (Warwick Library)

17. CAR 2

The tram at the front of the row of Leamington and Warwick trams appears to be Car 2, but with its arch-topped side windows it can only be one of the former Taunton trams renumbered at the very end of the existance of the system. The real car 2 should have had windows like the tram behind it in the gloom of Emscote depot. At the extreme rear of the depot can be made out the cut down works car, which survived the closure and was sold to Llandudno & Colwyn Bay Electric Railway. (J.H.Taylforth)

18. CAR 4

After the final closure of the electric tram system on Saturday 16 August 1930, the trams were driven to Emscote depot where they were dumped, some on the track and others on waste ground near to the Grand Union Canal.

Car 4 waits its fate, forelornly, in October 1930, some two months after the closure of the system. (S.L.Smith Collection)

19. UNIDENTIFIED BRUSH CAR

An unidentified Brush car from the 1 to 6 class has gone around Eastgate and is straightening up to run down Smith Street towards St Johns and Coten End in about 1910.

Eastgate was built in the early 15th Century, while the pinnacled chapel of St Peter was added in 1788. Next to it, in Smith Street is Landor House, where a workman is standing on a ladder doing some long forgotten repairs. The house is a timber framed, two-gabled building which was built in 1692, just two years before the Great Fire of Warwick. (Commercial Postcard)

20. CAR 2

The horse trams used to pass through the arch of the delightful Eastgate, but after the conversion to electric trams in 1905, this was impossible. The trams went from Jury Street and into Smith Street by way of the Castle Hill side of Eastgate.

Car 2 goes around the interlaced track on its way out of Warwick, while through the arch can be seen another one of the 1 to 6 class waiting in Smith Street, having come up the hill from St Johns. (Commercial Postcard)

21. CAR 2

The terminus in Warwick was in High Street at the stub section of track after a passing loop between Church Street, which led to St Marys Parish Church and Swan Street, which leads into the Market Place.

In about 1918, Brush-built open-topped, car 2, waits at the terminus with its crew posing on the platform. (Warwick Library)

22. CAR 14

Leamington & Warwick's most modern tramcar was number 14, there being no number 13 for obvious reasons! Car 14 had been built in 1921 for another member of the Balfour, Beatty Group. It should have been Cheltenham and District Light Railway's number 24, being the last of the four trams which they ordered; the others became Cheltenham and District's 21 to 23.

Car 14 was built by English Electric and cost £2,400. It had platform vestibules from new and had two 35 h.p. Metropolitan-Vickers motors. This made it nominally twice as powerful as anything else on the system.

This modern tram is standing in the terminal stub in High Street beneath the graceful Georgian buildings which line the street. These buildings were the replacements for those medieval wooden constructions within the confines of the old town walls which were destroyed in the Great Fire of 1694. (Whitcombe Collection)

23. Works Car

The only photograph which could be traced of the Leamington & Warwick works car, probably 11, was after it had been sold. The Gothic-arched windows identify this tram as one of the six ex-Taunton cars built by Brush in 1901 and purchased by the company four years later.

After the closure of the Leamington & Warwick system, this tram was purchased by the Llandudno & Colwyn Bay Electric Railway in 1930. It was used as their works car, numbered 23, until 1936 when a newer four-wheeler was purchased from Bournemouth Corporation as a replacement for the older tramcar. The former L. & W. works car is seen after withdrawal in Rhos depot. The body was later used as a store at Rhos depot. (Courtesy National Tramway Museum, Crich)

Leamington and Warwick Buses

1. O 1287

In October 1903, the Birmingham Motor Express Company began operation using three Napier 12 h.p. motor buses on the potentially lucrative Hagley Road route. By the early months of 1905, a new route to Harborne had been opened, again where there was no Corporation tramcar competition and B.M.E. had twenty buses in service.

On Thursday 1 June 1905, the recently registered Birmingham and Midland Motor Omnibus Company, (B.M.M.O.), took over all B.E.T. company operation in the city with an inherited fleet of Milnes-Daimlers, Durkopps and Wolseleys.

By the end of 1906, the new company had purchased nine Brush 'B' chassis which were fitted with 40 h.p. Mutel engines and were fitted with second-hand double-deck bodies from some of the earlier, by now withdrawn chassis. The buses were painted green and were registered O 1283-1291.

O 1287 is at the Ivy Bush, Hagley Road, Birmingham in 1907 carrying a full load. The popularity of B.M.M.O.'s Birmingham services, as demonstrated here with the overloaded Brush 'B', was not generally matched by the reliability of some of the other chassis marques. The B.E.T. Group had by this time seen-off any potential bus opposition; as their main operation was at that time based on the running of tramcars and there were problems with the efficiency of most of the motor buses, the decision was made to withdraw them with effect from Saturday, 5 October 1907.

All of the nine Brush 'B's were considered to be in good condition and six were sent on loan to a new B.E.T. operation in Deal with new Birch Brothers charabanc bodies. In March 1908 the remaining three, (O 1287, O 1289 and O 1290), went on hire to Leamington and Warwick and O 1287 was one of two which were fitted with new charabanc bodies. They were run on feeder services for the tramway and more importantly, on excursion work to Stratford-upon-Avon.

At this early stage, the link was forged between the tramway company and 'the distant town of Stratford'. (D.R.Harvey Collection)

2. UE 7087 and ex-Taunton tram

The Emscote tram depot catered for trams until as early as March 1908, when the three Birmingham-registered Brush 'B's, which were acquired by the Leamington & Warwick Company for local bus services as well as trips to Stratford, Banbury and Alcester, were also garaged at the site. The Great War put paid to bus operation by the then owners, British Automobile Traction Company. In order to protect their tram operation, Leamington & Warwick reintroduced buses in October 1927. This was in

response to the introduction of Stratford-upon-Avon Motor Services bus operation between Stratford, Warwick and Leamington. The first three buses were Tilling-Stevens B10Bs bought from Midland General, a subsidiary of the parent Balfour, Beatty.

In September 1928, three twenty-seater Reo FBXs were purchased and one of them, UE 7087, is parked near to an unidentified former Taunton tramcar built in 1901 and recently fitted with vestibule screens. The tram's advertisements for Thornleys Gold Medal Ales, Schweppes Tonic and Gillette razor blades seem today to be somewhat chauvinistic! (D.R.Harvey Collection)

3. 11, (UE 9326)

With the impending closure of the Leamington & Warwick trams, the company purchased two batches of six Daimler CF6s each with Brush B32F bodies in September 1929 and January 1930 respectively.

One of the first batch, 11, (UE 9326), stands in Leamington outside the splendidly named Empire Meat Company, on 11 May 1930, when about to work on the 'main route' to Warwick. The vertical panels above the windows hide the roof line and while aesthetically awful, did supply the company with advertising revenue. (Pamlin Prints)

4. 12, (UE 9324)

Daimler CF6, 12,(UE 9324), one of the six from the second batch of Brush-bodied buses, waits in Warwick on the service back to Leamington. These buses had relatively short lives, mostly being withdrawn in 1937, very soon after the take-over by Midland Red of the Leamington & Warwick Company. History would repeat itself in 1971, when a similar event caused the premature withdrawal of the Stratford Blue bus fleet! (D.R.Harvey Collection)

5. 16, (UE 9913)

The conductor winds the destination blind back as the bus slowly loads up in Warwick's Market Place. Brush-bodied Daimler CF6, 16, (UE 9913), painted in the attractive green and cream livery, entered service in January 1930 and for its time, was a handsome-looking machine, although beneath the surface, the design dated back to the mid-1920s. A presage of things to come is the Flower's Ales advertisement and what appears to be a silver roof. These would be two features which would soon become more familiar in association with blue and white colours in the nearby town of Stratford-upon-Avon. (C.F.Klapper)

Prewar Buses

Stratford-On-Avon Motor Services

1. Chevrolet LM and Thornycroft A2

Messrs Grail and Joiner began operation of their Stratford-opon-Avon Motor Services on 1 April 1927 with a fleet of Chevrolet LMs. There were initially seven of these small buses, all of which were fitted with Allen B14F bodies. The spindly single rear tyres would have been at their load limit when these little buses were fully loaded.

Their first route ran to Shottery, home of Ann Hathaway, William Shakespeare's wife. Her cottage, even in 1927, appears to have been a focal point in the village and as such was advertised on the side slipboard of Grail and Joiner's buses. The service had its terminus in Stratford in the Market Place. This was at the junction of Rother Street by the American Drinking Fountain which had been dedicated by the famous Victorian actor, Sir Henry Irving in 1887.

Behind the Chevrolet, with its driver and conductor wearing their smart white coats and caps, is one of the slightly larger Thornycroft A2s which entered service in 1928. (Shakespeare Guild Library)

2. 8, (UE 5283)

Typical of the Thornycroft A2s which Stratford-upon-Avon Motor Services bought is the first one 8, (UE 5283). It was built in 1928 and was fitted with a Park Royal twenty seat body. This gave a useful increase in the carrying capacity over the earlier Chevrolets of six seats. It is parked outside Ann Hathaway's Cottage in Shottery, which was the company's first route from Stratford. (R.Marshall)

The Balfour, Beatty Era

1. 19, (RA 3869)

The first foray into the Tiling-Stevens second-hand market came after the formation of the Stratford-upon-Avon Blue Motors under the ownership of the Balfour, Beatty Group. Running the Stratford operation from the Langley Mills headquarters of Midland General, it was quickly appreciated that larger vehicles were required. The result was the transfer of five assorted Tiling-Stevens, of which four were of the B9B normal-control variety.

The first of the quintet, 19, (RA 3869), had a Brush B30F body and dated from 1927. The five went to Stratford Blue in 1931 and served for five years before being replaced by second-hand forward-control Tiling-Stevens. 19 is seen parked outside the travel bureau in Cheltenham about 1934. (M.Rooum)

2. (UE 9816)

When the Reliance Bus Company of Bidford-on-Avon was taken over by Stratford Blue in 1932, two Star V4s were retained. These Wolverhampton-built twenty seaters were fitted with a 3.2 litre petrol engine which were known for their 50 m.p.h. top speed. Surprisingly, two Guy ONDs with Guy B20F bodies built in 1930 were transferred to the Balfour, Beatty-owned Cheltenham District without entering service in the Bard's town.

1, (UE 9816), is seen in Cheltenham, not long after being transferred to Cheltenham District, as it was later renumbered 18. (C.F.Klapper)

3. (UE 9319)

The second Guy OND taken over by Stratford Blue from Reliance was UE 9319. In retrospect, it was a surprising decision to get rid of Reliance's pair of Guy ONDs to Cheltenham District and to keep the two Star V4s. The decision to purchase four of the larger second-hand Guy "Conquest" Cs, which travelled in the opposite direction in 1934, therefore seemed even more peculiar.

The little Guy OND competed with smaller types of buses such as the Dennis G, Chevrolet and the Morris Commercial 30cwt. UE 9319 was originally numbered 2 by Cheltenham District but was renumbered 19. It is operating on the 5 service to Sandy Lane and its conductor stands on the pavement shepherding passengers on to the bus. Behind it is Cheltenham District 14, (DF 8906), a splendid open-topped Guy FC. (G.S.Lloyd)

4. — (DG 1313)

The last vehicles acquired by Stratford-upon-Avon Blue Motors in the period of ownership by the Balfour, Beatty Group were four normal-control Guy "Conquest" 'C' types, built in 1930. They were numbered 14-16 and 20. They were massive looking vehicles whose bonnets contained a six-cylinder petrol engine which seemed to take up almost a third of the length of the vehicles. The rest of the bus body only seated 28!

The four Guys were purchased from Cheltenham District in 1934, but only remained in service until the first of the Tilling-Stevens B10A2s were bought. DG 1313, an identical vehicle to the four transferred to Stratford-upon-Avon Blue Motors is working in the centre of Cheltenham as their 20. (M.Rooum)

5. 22, (WD 3338)

In 1932, an unusual choice of demonstrator was operated by Stratford Blue. It was an Albion "Valiant" PV70, which had been introduced the previous year. It was fitted with a 6.03 litre six-cylinder petrol engine. Albion Motors of Scotstoun, Glasgow, even went to the trouble of registering their vehicle in Warwickshire. 22, (WD 3338), was fitted with an unusual choice of bodywork for a bus. The Albion had a Harrington B32F body; Thomas Harrington were better known as coachbuilders, so that one of their fairly rare bus bodies fitted with an uncommon chassis south of the Border was indeed a rare sight. The Albion is loading up with passengers at Stratford-upon-Avon railway station when on hire.

The following year, Stratford Blue had another demonstrator; this time it was an A.E.C. "Regal" 662, 23, (AMD 739), again with a Harrington body, only this time it was a coach body. Again, Stratford Blue did not 'bother the manufacturers' for orders. (C.F.Klapper)

Midland Red Assume Control
The Tilling-Stevens Era

6. 12, (VT 580)

The first of many Tilling-Stevens B10A2s to be purchased by Stratford Blue after the take-over by Midland Red from the Balfour, Beatty Group was 12, (VT 580), which was one of a pair bought from Trent Motor Traction which in turn had acquired them from 'Kingfisher', a Derby-based independent.

As with virtually everything else purchased by Stratford Blue about this time, it was not quite as straight forward as it appeared. Not only were the two buses third-hand, but they had recently been rebodied by Willowbrook with a modern-looking B32F body. Even more surprisingly, VT 580, probably because of its new body, was one of the last B10A2s to remain in service. It is parked in the Stratford Blue garage yard on 30 April 1950, not long before it was withdrawn from service in favour of the new PS2/3s. (C.W.Heaps)

7. 21, (DB 5166)

One of the first block second-hand purchases by Stratford Blue was of eighteen Tilling-Stevens B10A2s. They were new to North Western Road Car Company in 1928, but again the batch were not quite the same. Seven of the vehicles had eight-bay construction Brush B36R bodies, while the remaining eleven had Tilling B32R bodies.

The last one of the group was 21, (DB 5166). It had a chassis design which was distinctly a product of the 1920s, emphasised by the high steering position and the bulb-horn sticking through the front cab panel. 21 was converted to a tree-lopper and survived until 1952 when it was replaced by DB 9380. It is parked in the Stratford garage yard on 30 April 1950 in front of 12, (VT 580). (C.W.Heaps)

29

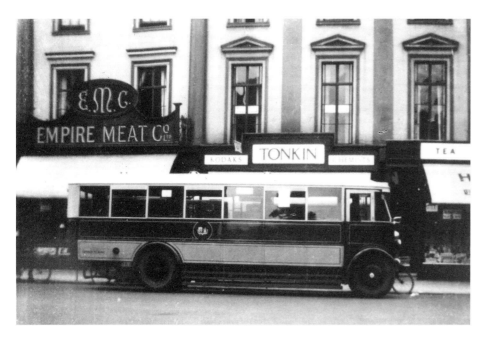

8. 23. (UE 9323)

Leamington and Warwick 9, (UE 9323), waits in the Parade, Royal Leamington Spa, at the stop outside the well-known Empire Meat Company butchers shop. The bus is an almost new Daimler CF6, which entered service in September 1929. It is fitted with an attractive Brush B32F body that would later be spoilt by having all-round roof advertisement boards.

The Daimler CF6 used Daimler's own 5.76 litre sleeve-valve six-cylinder engine, which although was splendidly smooth was also characterised by its gentle plume of blue exhaust smoke. The chassis had a cone-type clutch which was already becoming a dated feature as the new John Rackham designed A.E.C. "Regal" and Leyland "Tiger" models both had plate clutches. The Daimler CF6 was the last bus chassis produced by the Coventry company to have a short, very 1920s type radiator. To some extent, the CF6 was a transitional model between the A.D.C vehicles built up to 1928 and the COG range introduced in 1933.

It was for these reasons that CF6s were a short-lived breed and the Leamington and Warwick buses were no exception. In 1937, this bus, UE 9323 was sold to Stratford Blue as their number 9, but still only remained in service for another twelve months. (D.R.Harvey Collection)

9. 9, (WX 2125)

Later to become Stratford Blue 9, WX 2125, on its spindly tyres, passes through Bolton Abbey arch. It is in its original condition with West Yorkshire Road Car as their 258 and is fitted with metal-plate bible-board destination boxes. After acquision in October 1938, these boards were replaced by destination boxes fitted beneath the canopy. (West Yorkshire Information Service)

10. 10, (WX 2130)

Whizzing through Stratford at Bridge Street on 20 April 1939 is a United-bodied Tilling-Stevens B10A2, 10, (WX 2130). This had entered service with West Yorkshire Road Car Company as their 274 from their Leeds garage in July 1930. It had been purchased by Stratford Blue only six months before this photograph was taken and had been one of sixteen buses taken over. Although the United body had been rebuilt by West Yorkshire in August 1935, the overall look of the vehicle remained distinctly old-fashioned with its tall, high body combined to the low-set Tilling-Stevens bonnet line. (J.Cull)

11. 4, (WX 2134)

Long journeys on a Tilling-Stevens B10A2 today would be considered to be something of a challenge, but in 1932, West Yorkshire's 278, (WX 2134), fitted with a United B32F body is working on the long Leeds, Tadcaster, York and Beverley service.

The B10A2 waits in Rougier Street, York, beneath the York Corporation tram wires. In October 1938 this bus became Stratford Blue's 4. It is at the head of a wonderful array of vehicles including a West Yorkshire Leyland "Tiger" TS1 531, (WX 5922) and an elderly A.D.C. 415A of United Automobile which is working the route from Ripon. (West Yorkshire Information Service)

12. 4, (WX 2134)

The last batch of second-hand vehicles purchased by Stratford Blue before the Second World War were a further sixteen Tilling-Stevens B10A2s in October 1938. Unlike the previous buses, these came from West Yorkshire Road Car Company. The chassis dated from between February and May 1930 and again these buses had B32F bodies constructed by three different bodybuilders. Six had Tilling bodies, including this one, 4, (WX 2134) and with larger side windows, they were a more upto-date six-bay construction body. It is parked in the garage yard in Stratford.

In the rest of the batch there were seven vehicles bodied by United and three by Roe. (R.Marshall Collection)

13. 14, (WX 2118)

This official United photograph shows West Yorkshire Road Car 262, (WX 2118), when new in February 1930. The Tilling-Stevens B10A2 chassis frame was quite low, comparing favourably with other manufacturers products. This enabled modern-looking bodies to be built on the Tilling-Stevens chassis, though the rear end treatment by United was redolent of designs of a few years earlier.

The problem with the vehicles were on the mechanical side as their 70 b.h.p. four-cylinder petrol engines were derived from those introduced by Tilling-Stevens about 1926. The low, thick-set radiator meant that from the front, the vehicles looked old-fashioned even when they were new. This bus became Stratford Blue's 14 and lasted until May 1948. (D.R.Harvey Collection)

14. 16, (WX 2144)

At the other end of its career is another of the ex-West Yorkshire Road Car Tilling-Stevens B10A2 built in 1930 with a United B32F body. This was Stratford Blue 16, (WX 2144) and was withdrawn by them in November 1948. It became a showman's vehicle being used as a caravan. By the mid-1950s, it was still roadworthy and other than being fitted with a chimney, was still basically complete. (A.D.Broughall)

15. 19, (WX 2150)

The final state of dereliction! 19, (WX 2150), one of the Roe B32F bodied Tilling-Stevens B10A2s that had formerly been West Yorkshire Road Car 294, had served Stratford Blue for ten years and two months.

It was sold to Robert Fossett who ran it as a circus vehicle until October 1953. Then it was abandoned. Even in this state, the traditional Charles Roe raised waistrail can still be seen. (A.D.Broughall)

16. 22, (JO 2354)

The first double-decker operated by Stratford Blue was purchased in March 1940. The war-time needs of the company were hard pressed as within their operating were a number of large R.A.F. bases including the large base at nearby Wellesbourne. Although buses were in fairly short supply by 1940, the company's buying policy was as strange during the war as it was before the outbreak of hostilities.

A motley collection of hired vehicles were operated, in a number of cases, until years after the war had ended, but only JO 2354 was actually purchased. This had been G167 in the City of Oxford Motor Services fleet and was given the Stratford Blue fleet number 22. It was a 1931

A.E.C."Regent" 661, i.e. petrol-engined and had a Park Royal H24/24R composite body of distinctly square proportions. 22 remained in service until March 1948 being replaced when the GUE-registered Leyland "Titan" PD2/1s entered service.

The vehicle in the photograph is sister bus G170, (JO 2392), operating in Oxford for its original owner. Unfortunately the only known photograph of JO 2354 operating is so indistinct as to make it unuseable. (Oxford Bus Museum)

17. 20, (DB 9375)

Immediately after the Second World War, in 1946, Stratford Blue again entered the second-hand market and for the third time, purchased more Tilling-Stevens chassis, again dating from 1930.

Eight vehicles were purchased from North Western Road Car Company, only this time they had been rebodied by Eastern Counties in 1935 with B31R bodies that were virtually the same as those supplied to North Western on new Bristol JO5G chassis.

20, (DB 9375), is parked in Stratford Blue's garage yard in 1949 and shows off the old-fashioned starting handle, low-mounted radiator and almost cycle-style front wings. (D. R. Harvey Collection)

18. 21, (DB 9377)

One of the eight Tilling-Stevens B10A2s bought in 1946 was 21, (DB 9377). It is parked in Stratford Blue's garage yard and has its radiator and bonnet covered with a large muff to protect it against frost damage on cold winter nights.

These vehicles were only kept for about four years, for although they were fitted with E.C.O.C. bodies dating from 1935, their chassis were sixteen years old when purchased. They all succumbed to the final influx of new Leyland "Tiger" PS2 in 1950. (R.Marshall)

19. 26, (DB 9395)

Hovis wholemeal brown bread is still with us today, but the receipient of the advertisement disappeared half a century ago. 26, (DB 9395), is parked in the garage yard at Stratford having been photographed for advertising purposes.

A number of details about these buses are note-worthy in this unusual rear view. Beneath the rear window are the two brackets for a slip-board. At the bottom of the rear panel, it is licensed to have 31 seats - though on market days, these old single-deckers were frequently "loaded to the gunwales".

Sporting what appears to be a new rear number plate, following this bus along a narrow Warwickshire lane on a dark, moonless night would not have been much fun. Just look for the only rear light -ouch! (Shakespeare Guild Library)

20. 27, (DB 9368)

One of the last survivors of the 'Tilling-Stevens'-era was 27, (DB 9368). It is parked in the garage yard on 30 April 1950, still smartly painted, but looking a little battered around the edges. Both front wings show signs of having arguments with the other objects, while the body, which by this time was fifteen years old, is beginning to sag, suggesting that all is not well underneath the panels.

Despite its age, 27 was still being used on the longer routes, such as the one to Evesham, even though almost new Leyland single-deckers were both available and a much better proposition. (C.W.Heaps)

21. 30, (DB 9389)

Despite their elderly chassis, the Stratford Blue company maintained the Tilling-Stevens vehicles remarkably well. 30, (DB 9389), is parked in the garage yard in the summer of 1947. The lined out livery on the E.C.O.C. body is extremely smart and the bus appears to have benefitted from a new set of front wings. The new bodies were very well appointed inside having virtually dual-purpose seats which were extremely comfortable. Only the rattling of the hard pushed petrol engine would have spoilt the passenger's ride.

30 was the penultimate Tilling-Stevens bus of the batch of eight to be purchased by Stratford Blue from North Western in 1946. It had formerly been number 489 in the N.W.R.C. fleet. (J.H.Taylforth Collection)

L.M.S. Ro-Railer

Although not a Stratford Blue vehicle, in the town there was briefly operated another 'bus' which is worthy of mention. In 1932, this vehicle would have been the most modern half-bus to grace the streets of Stratford-upon-Avon and yet it was deemed a failure. Throughout the late 1920s and early 1930s, a number of attempts were made to produce a railcar, powered by the internal combustion engine. One of the by-products of these progressions were attempts to introduce a vehicle that would be able to run on road and rail with equal facility. Various attempts were made to convert buses to either this dual use, or as in the case of the Great Northern Railway of Ireland to convert them to what effectively were primitive railcars. Probably the most famous attempt to produce a convertible road-rail vehicle was that made by the London Midland Scottish Railway with their Ro-Railer. They recognised that an attempt to make branch-lines more profitable could be made by developing the road-rail concept. In the end the experiment turned out to be a blind alley and although trial runs were tried out in a blaze of publicity in 1932, the whole concept was quickly abandoned.

1. (UR 7924)

The vehicle demonstrated by the L.M.S. railway was a Karrier "Chaser" chassis with a Craven B26C body. The choice of Karrier was unusual, in that by 1931, when the chassis was built, Karrier motor bus production was virtually at an end. The last 'throw of the dice' as far as Karrier P.S.V.s were concerned were the double-deck "Consort" and the single-deck "Chaser". Neither was a success as the poor reputation of the six-wheeled Karrier buses of the late 1920s went before them.

Cravens-Tasker, the railway carriage and wagon builder, periodically dabbled in the bus and tram market, famously for its post-war non-standard RT-type bodies for London Transport.

The 'Ro-Railer' was registered in Hertfordshire as UR 7924 and worked initially on the Redbourn branch near Hemel Hempstead. It was later transferred to work from Stratford and is leaving Stratford station to travel in bus mode to the Welcombe Hotel on the south side of Clopton Bridge. The rail wheels can just be seen glinting inside the front nearside tyre. (Stratford Guild Library)

2. (UR 7924)

The Karrier 'Ro-Railer' waits at the busy platform of the former L.N.W.R. Stratford station, having metamorphosed itself into a railbus. Behind UR 7924, opposite the signal box, is where the vehicle was driven onto the rails and the rail wheels lowered onto the track. The road wheels were then jacked-up in a procedure which took about three minutes to effect.

UR 7924 was employed on the branch-line from Stratford to Blisworth and the experiment for several weeks began on 23 April 1932, appropriately enough Shakespeare's birthday.

It was a shame that the idea did not work. The concept could have been operated successfully, but undoubtedly bus operators would have seen this vehicle as a

potential threat to their already marginal profits on rural routes. The dubious reliability of the Karrier meant that the true railcar concept as developed so successfully by the Great Western Railway was inevitably going to be the way forward as far as rail-bus development was concerned. (Stratford Guild Library)

War-Time Buses

1. 1032, (HA 4942)

The remains of Stratford Blue's only Midland Red-built vehicle bought for service was 1032, (HA 4942). It lies derelict in a yard in Towyn.

After service with Stratford Blue, 1032 was returned to Midland Red and was used as a mobile workshop for a few years. The remnants of this S.O.S. 'M'-type reveals the structure of the very lightweight Ransomes, Simms and Jefferies body. The characteristic of most of B.M.M.O.'s pre-war vehicles was the location of the fuel tank beneath the driver's seat. Casualties were surprisingly few! (Vectis Transport)

2. 1024, (HA 4937)

The Ransomes-bodied S.O.S. 'M' "Madam" which was purchased by Stratford Blue was never photographed in service with the company. A similar vehicle, 1024, (HA 4937), is seen on familiar stamping ground in Banbury in early post-war days. As Stratford Blue worked into Banbury, this at least shows what HA 4942 would have looked like in its Stratford Blue operating area. (R. H. G. Simpson)

3. 1675, (AHA 619)

During the Second World War, the parent company hired out to Stratford Blue a number of vehicles. One of these was Midland Red's 1675, (AHA 619).

Beauty, they say, is in the eye of the beholder and no one could dispute that the S.O.S. OLR was an impressive looking normal control vehicle. It had a canvas topped Short Brothers C29F and despite being built as late as 1935, was a direct successor to the charabancs of the late 1920s, without actually being one. AHA 619 was converted to forward control in 1941 as a war-time measure to utilise the available fleet for the best results. It was hired by Stratford Blue from 1945 until 1948 and was given the fleet number 26. After it was returned to Midland Red it ran in service until 1952. It is seen in its original condition parked in Bradford Street outside the former premises of bus body builder, John Buckingham, when new in 1935. (J.Cull)

4. 1677, (AHA 622)

This low-radiatored bus, with its modern, sleek front wings, at first sight looks like a typical half-cab single-decker, though admittedly, with a more generously sized cab than the normal Midland Red pre-war single-deckers.

But this was all a cunning ploy to create extra buses from the fleet of pre-war coaches. The low height of the rest of the body of AHA 622 gives a clue as to this vehicles origins. It is an S.O.S. OLR, which had been converted from a canvas-roofed coach into a forward-control B34F bus in 1941. It is included here because this was what 1675, (AHA 619), looked like when it was hired to Stratford Blue in 1945. It is parked in Acocks Green, Birmingham in about 1950 and is about to leave on the short suburban route to Yardley. (D.Barlow)

The Stratford Blue car hire fleet of Humber "Pullman's" should have really been Stratford Black!

The Humber "Pullman" was in production between 1948 and 1954.

These limousines were almost as long as a small bus being 17' 6" long. They had six or seven seats and the Pullman was propelled by a 4086cc six-cylinder side valve engine.

Apparently even with the later ohv engine of 4138cc, they were a morticious delight - black and exceedingly dull to drive.

Postwar Buses 1948-1956

1. 33, (GUE 239)

Standing in rural Warwickshire between Alcester and Great Alne near the hamlet of Kinwarton at harvest time, is Leyland "Titan" PD2/1, 33, (GUE 239). The classic lines of the Colin Bailey-designed Leyland metal-framed body, even after about ten years in service, are evident in this posed photograph. By this time, in the late 1950s, the livery had changed slightly as the black lining out had been omitted, though the almost statutory advertisement for the products of the local Flowers brewery remained as an almost integral part of the livery.

33 was the second of eight PD2/1s delivered in March 1948 and must have been a revelation to the good folk of Stratford who had been used for far too many years to the elderly Tilling-Stevens single-deckers. (D.R.Harvey Collection)

2. 34, (GUE 240)

The garage at Kineton had been inherited with the purchase of the Kineton Green bus fleet on 1 January 1937 and was usually occupied by a cross-section of the Stratford Blue fleet. On Sunday 30 April 1950, Leyland-bodied PD2/1 34, (GUE 240), stands on the forecourt of the garage with the driver and conductor sitting in the lower saloon. Presumably they are waiting before taking up their duties on the 524 service. On Sundays this service went from Stratford to Evesham in about 80 minutes and one of the villages the route passed through was Quinton.

The bus is painted in its original blue and white livery with black-lining out, black livery bands and black mudguards, topped off with a silver painted-roof. Perhaps the only disappointing feature of these original eight PD2/1s was that their radiators were also painted blue. At this time Leyland's offered a variety of finishes to their radiators which could be chromed, aluminium and, as specified by quite a large number of operators, painted either in black or to match the fleet livery. At least the Stratford Blue radiators had a certain degree of individuality. (C.Heaps)

3. 35, (GUE 241)

When the joint-working service to Birmingham was introduced on 31 May 1952, the obvious candidates to operate the service were the Leyland double-deckers of 1948 and 1950, as they all had seating capacities of 56. Any doubts about operating the service with double-deckers were dispelled when it was realised that the canal aqueduct at Wootten Wowen and the railway bridge at Bearley, both plated at 14' 3", (which usually allowed another 6" clearance) had been negotiated by the Midland Red FEDD double-deckers which were officially about 14' 7". The standard Leyland highbridge body was only 14' 4 7/8" and as a result of them being able to work through the bridges quite comfortably, they were a welcome, modern addition to the 150 route.

On 3 August 1953, 35, (GUE 241), waits in Jamaica Row alongside St Martin's Parish Church at the edge of Birmingham's market area. It is in company with one of the three brand new MAC-registered Leyland "Titan" PD2/12s bought specifically to run on the prestigious 150 joint service with Midland Red. (D.R.Harvey Collection)

4. 36, (GUE 242) / 23, (MAC 570)

The Red Lion bus station on the corner of Bridge Foot and Warwick Road was opposite the Stratford Blue garage which is visible in the distance. These two sites were the hub of the company's operations and as such was a hive of activity.

In this late 1950s view, 36, (GUE 242), one of the 1948 PD2/1s is parked next to 23, (MAC 570), the first of the trio of the longer PD2/12s delivered in 1952. The difference between the Leyland bodies, as they had developed in the ensuing five years between 1948 and 1953 had resulted in the perhaps more aggressive styling of the earlier vehicle giving way to the more rounded window pans and the omission of the front guttering on MAC 570. This latter design had been introduced in 1951 when the 27' long, 8' wide, PD2/12 had been introduced.

The livery style had been simplified on the PD2/12 with the upper-deck cream band being omitted. The Balfour, Beatty/B.E.T-style Clayton externally opening front destination box was also replaced, giving way to the more orthodox rubber-mounted display aperture. The opening box, seen on 36, had the advantage that replacement blinds could be fitted from the outside. This was done by simply moving the external catch, which is just visible below the word 'GREEN' on the blind lettering which enabled the complete box to be opened to gain access to the blind.

Parked at the back of the bus station is a Midland Red, Duple-bodied C1 coach while behind the passing Bedford C4 van, in the entrance to the Stratford Blue garage is a Willowbrook-bodied Leyland "Tiger Cub", a JUE-registered PD2/1 and one of the Willowbrook-bodied Leyland "Tiger" PS2/3s of 1950.

Just to disprove everything mentioned previously about the GUE-batch of PD2/1s, 36 is sporting a polished aluminium radiator, rather than the original blue-painted one and probably looks all the better for it! (A.J.Douglas)

5. 37, (GUE 243)

Rear views of double-deckers are never common, but this photograph of 37, (GUE 243) is doubly interesting. The photograph was taken in 1948 when the bus was only a few months old to show potential advertisers what was available for advertisement space between the decks and below the rear platform window.

The view also shows the legal lettering for the seating capacity and the one single red rear side-light alongside the illuminated rear number plate box. The platform served as the nearside equivalent, though of course this was white and not red. After 1956 when the Construction and Use Regulations were altered, two red rear lights were required. In the gap between the letters GUE and the numbers 243 is a small hyphen-like dash. This carried the legend 'SIMS LIGHT Patentees, Bolton' in very small letters. The whole number-plate was illuminated red at night and was an additional rear light marker for use after dark.

The light was a standard Leyland postwar fixture used until about 1950 when they were replaced by normal white number-plates. (Stratford Birthplace Trust)

6. 43, (GUE 249)

The Northern Coach Builders-bodied Leyland "Tiger" PS1s were unique as a batch of vehicles. N.C.B. only ever built eleven single-deckers buses after it had courted the B.E.T. Group for orders. The prototype was delivered to Yorkshire Traction and should have been the first of twenty such bodies going to that operator. Production difficulties at Newcastle resulted in Yorkshire Traction cancelling the balance of the contract. N.C.B. had eventually laid in parts for some of the rest of the order and had enough parts to construct a further ten single-deck bodies. These materialised as Stratford Blue's 40-49 batch.

43, (GUE 249), is parked on Kineton's garage forecourt on 30 April 1950 basically in its "as delivered" condition. Perhaps the only disappointing aspect of the design was the rather 'home-made' looking windscreen area. The styling of these B.E.T. "Federation" bodies was, elsewhere, most attractive. The saloon windows, although totally non-standard N.C.B., were well proportioned and not unlike those being put in contemporary Brush bodies. (C.Heaps)

7. 44, (GUE 250)

The passengers on the half-full single-decker 44, (GUE 250), wait for their driver and conductor before leaving the Red Lion bus station at Bridge Foot on the 31 service to Cornbrook.

These ten N.C.B.-bodied Leyland "Tiger PS1s were the first new single-deckers purchased by the company since the days of Stratford-upon-Avon Motor Services. They proved to be good investment for the company. They replaced the antiquated Tilling-Stevens vehicles bought in 1946 from North Western Road Car, and enabled the acceleration of service frequency and timings while giving Stratford Blue a much better up-to-date image in the town. By the mid-1950s the boom in travel and tourism meant that Stratford-upon-Avon, (spoken in a broad U.S. of A.-type drawl!), with its Shakespearean connections, became a 'honey-pot' centre for visitors. Rattling old buses just would not have done anything to enhance the town, while the new, smart blue and white buses complimented the more traditional appearance of the town and gave the impression of a business-like transport operation. (R.Marshall)

8. 52, (JUE 350) / 53, (JUE 351) / 30, (DB 9389)

The second batch of single-deckers delivered to Stratford Blue after the war were two bus-bodied Leyland "Tiger" PS2/1s and four dual-purpose-bodied Leyland "Tiger" PS2/3s. Two of these four semi-coaches are parked in the Stratford Blue garage yard. They are 52, (JUE 350) and 53, (JUE 351) and are seen when only a few weeks old. The "Tiger" PS2/3s were fitted with Willowbrook DP34F bodies, which differed from the buses by having a drop-rear frame chassis extention which allowed them to be fitted with a rear luggage boot.

With their large 9.8 litre Leyland 0.600 engines, they were a much better proposition for private hire and excursion work than the 7.4 litre E181 engined PS1s of two years earlier.

Hidden in the shadow of the tree at the back of the garage yard is one of the few Tilling-Stevens B10A2s, bought from North Western Road Car in 1946, that survived to see the PS2s come into service. The Tilling-Stevens is 30, (DB 9389), a vehicle whose 1930 chassis was rebodied by Eastern Counties in 1935. (B.W.Ware Collection)

9. 54, (JUE 352)

The Willowbrook bus-bodied Leyland "Tiger" PS2/1s were used for the longer stage carriage routes such as the three services operated from Kineton to North Bar in Banbury. 54, (JUE 352), destined to be the only one of the six PS2s not to be rebodied as a double-decker, waits to load up with more passengers in Banbury in the mid-1950s before making the 55 minute journey back to Kineton. Parked with the bus are a couple of Bedford SB-type coaches which had become so popular with rural operators about this time. The Stratford Blue bus was one of the pair of bus

bodies supplied by Willowbrook which were only a less-well appointed version of the four dual-purpose vehicles. Externally, the only difference was the lack of the cream swoop on the lower saloon side panels. (R.H.G.Simpson)

10. 52, (JUE 350) / 51, (JUE 349)

The half-cab single-decker reigned supreme until about 1950, when both A.E.C. with their "Regal" IV and Leyland, with their "Royal Tiger" underfloor engined P.S.V. chassis began to make heavy inroads into the previously standard front-engined layout for single-deckers.

For example, in 1950 when the sextet of Stratford Blue PS2s was delivered, a total of 318 Leyland PS2s were purchased by bus and coach operators in the U.K. Yet only two years later, only 22 PS2s were supplied within the U.K., with West Riding in Wakefield having 18 of them.

For many operators, especially coach companies, after about five or six years of use, what had been the pride of the fleet in 1949-50 had become as antiquated as the charabanc of twenty-five years earlier. The sleek-bodied underfloor engined coaches, could accommodate more passengers than the half-cab, though it has to be said, some bodybuilders products were anything but sleek; over-elaborate and clumsy come frequently to mind. The result was that by the end of the 1950s there was a glut of second-hand half-cab coaches into a market which had little use for them. Large numbers of such coaches ended up in scrapyards long before they were time expired. A similar situation existed with half-cab buses, though the single-deck bus could expect to get through to the end of its second seven year Certificate of Fitness.

In Northern Ireland, the Ulster Transport Authority rebuilt 158 single-deck buses from PS2/1s to PD2/10c specification and with their c.k.d.-M.C.C.W./U.T.A. double-deck bodies gave about fifteen years extra service in their new guise. Yorkshire Traction rebuilt 24 of their PS2/3s between 1961 and 1963 with either Northern Counties or Charles Roe double-deck bodies.

The Stratford Blue management obviously decided that their PS2 chassis also had some life left in them and took PS2/1, 53, (JUE 353), out of service. Its body was scrapped and it received a new, rather ungainly, top-heavy looking forward entrance body built by Charles Roe of Crossgates, Leeds in 1961. The theory was fine but the practice looked awful and Roe were never asked to build another body for Stratford Blue!

The four PS2/3s were withdrawn from service in 1962 and were sent away to Yorkshire Traction, who after disposing of the redundant Willowbrook bodies, sent the refurbished chassis to Northern Counties. The Wigan-based company made a much better 'fist' of the job than the desperate job done at Crossgates, producing four very attractive bodies.

52, (JUE 350) and 51, (JUE 349), stand in a Yorkshire scrapyard on 24 June 1962 apparently 'lost and forlorn', though in actual fact, the panels have been removed, not as a prelude to breaking-up, but to allow the surplus single-deck bodies to be lifted from the chassis, prior to being taken away to be prepared for life as a double-decker. (G.Holt)

11. 27, (JUE 355)

Waiting alongside the Red Lion public house in September 1954 in the bus station is Leyland "Titan" PD2/1, 27, (JUE 355). This was one of five Leyland-bodied double-deckers which were purchased in 1950 and is still in its original style of lined-out livery.

These buses had the more attractive aluminium radiator shell which considerably enhanced their appearance. Compared with the GUE-registered batch, the detailed styling of the Leyland bodies had been modified; the removal of the guttering above the front upper saloon windows gave the buses a more modern look and tidied up the front end of the design. The

JUEs had rather unattractive square-topped sliding ventilators rather than the half-drops of the earlier batch.

This solitary bus is standing alongside the bus timetable notice whose position at the exit to the bus station on the small 'island' of pavement, always seemed terribly exposed and vulnerable to damage from departing buses. Interested intending passengers were also apparently at great risk. (R.Knibbs)

12. 30, (JUE 358)

The JUE-batch of Leyland-bodied Leylands were standard production examples of the then current style being built at the Farington works. 30, (JUE 358), stands on the stone cobbles in Birmingham's Bull Ring in front of St Martin's church on Sunday 14 April 1957, having just arrived from Stratford on the 150 service. In front of the Leyland is a Midland Red FEDD whose Brush body had been renovated about seven years earlier and which made the bodies look even taller.

The 1950 PD2/1s were the last Stratford Blue buses to have the Clayton opening front destination

box. The destination blind reveals that Stratford Blue was very much the junior partner on the joint service as it reads 'STRATFORD-UPON-AVON - ON HIRE TO MIDLAND RED'. This was because the service was licensed to Midand Red

It is a good thing that there were no April showers on this particular Sunday as the utility bus shelters would not have given any intending passengers much protection. (D.R.Harvey Collection)

13. 24, (MAC 571), /4067, (SHA 467), /4759, (759 BHA)

And not a bus bound for Birmingham! The line-up of buses operating out of the Red Lion bus station has Stratford Blue 24, (MAC 571) working on the 44 service through to Oxford on a joint service with City of Oxford Motor Services. Standing next to it is 4067, (SHA 467), which is about to go to Leamington Spa via Wellesbourne on the 518 route. The bus nearest to the timetable noticeboard is one of the last of the B.M.M.O. D7s to be built, 4759, (759 BHA), which is on the 524 service to Evesham via Broadway.

Both the Leyland "Titans" are PD2/12, though SHA 467 is one of the one hundred built with the concealed radiator that was designed specifically for Midland Red. The B.M.M.O. D7 shows how the contemporary 'home-built' version had been developed. The Leyland version of the Midland Red front was eventually offered onto the general market at the end of 1954. By that time, Leyland Motors had ceased body building, which left the Midland Red PD2/12s unique as the only new tin-fronted Leyland-bodied Leylands to enter P.S.V. service. (D.R.Harvey Collection)

14. 25, (MAC 572)

The three 27' long Leyland "Titan" PD2/12s had the final version of the Leyland Farington body and were the first 8' wide buses in the fleet. They were H32/26R layout and were fitted with saloon heaters and very soon after their delivery, doors. These MAC-registered vehicles entered service in May 1952 to coincide with the start of the joint working with Midland Red to Birmingham. The main improvement in this last type of Leyland body was the use of deep-set window pans which produced a more modern effect. 25, (MAC 572), waits in the Red Lion bus station which is carrying, rather anonymously the obvious destination STRATFORD-ON-AVON on both blinds. (S.N.J.White)

15. 56, (OUE 11)

For the start of the 1954 "Season", Stratford Blue purchased its first true coaches with the intention of opening up its excursion business. The coaches, which arrived in April 1954, were a pair of heavyweight Leyland "Royal Tiger" PSU1/16s and fitted with Burlingham "Seagull" C37C bodies. While the body style became something as a classic as far as coach designs were concerned, the "Royal Tiger", Leyland's first essay into underfloor engined single-deckers proved to be an expensive luxury. Most of the early underfloor engined chassis were grossly over-engineered, resulting in very heavy chassis.

When coupled to a coach body, the end product weighed more than the normal double-decker service bus.

The first of the twins, 56, (OUE11), waits for passengers who have, no doubt, taken the opportunity to avail themselves of the refreshment facilities in the adjacent cafe.

In the 1950s, before car ownership became almost obligatory, 'coaching' was still something special and an adventure for the passengers. There was a certain pride in the vehicles which dated back to an earlier time; echoes of this pride can be seen in the attention to detail as is shown with the regiment of perfectly straight, monogrammed antimacassars. (D.R.Harvey Collection)

16. 20, (TNX 454)

Although still able to purchase the exposed-radiatored, 8' wide PD2/12 model, fitted with a synchromesh - gearbox and vacuum-brakes as late as 1956, the year before it went out of production, the Leyland body was unavailable and therefore a new bodybuilder had to be found. Stratford Blue turned to Willowbrook, who were based in Loughborough, to body their next three double-deckers. They were the first four-bay bodied 'deckers in the fleet and with an H35/28RD seating layout, sat five more than the previous batch of Leyland-bodied Leylands.

The design was beginning to follow the trend towards lighter bodywork, with a less luxurious specification helping to reduce fuel costs. The rather upright front dome with the ventilators recessed in the upper saloon windows, gave these buses a slightly ungainly look.

20, (TNX 454), stands in the Red Lion bus station on 6 August 1969, painted in the simplified final version of the blue and white livery and the lower case fleet names. Further economies have resulted in the blanking out of the destination box above the entrance. (D.J.Little)

Post-War Buses 1957-1971

1. 43, (2744 AC)

The first underfloor-engined buses were purchased in 1959 and were of the "lightweight" type. These were the second generation of the type and had smaller Leyland 0.350 5.7 litre engines; this in turn resulted in fuel consumption figures in excess of 15 m.p.g. Stratford Blue ordered four Leyland "Tiger Cub" PSUC1/1 and these were bodied as 41-seater dual-purpose vehicles by Willowbrook. Their bodies were to the then standard B.E.T.-style, with a recessed driver's windscreen while the large front apron was embellished with a large chromed, winged motif.

The fourth vehicle of the batch, 43, (2744 AC), stands at the Red Lion bus station prior to departing to the nearby village of Loxley, when fairly new. (R.Marshall)

2. 48. (3948 UE)

For their second batch of dual-purpose single-deckers, Stratford Blue turned for the only time to Park Royal for their bodywork. Every year, the B.E.T. group allocated their single-deck body orders to usually two or three selected bodybuilders. In 1960, Park Royal, an infrequent choice for single-deck buses received a share in the B.E.T. contract and Stratford Blue received their bodies as part of the share out of deliveries.

Although following the basic outline of the previous Willowbrook-bodied "Tiger Cub" PSUC1/1s, the 45-48 batch were 45 seaters. 48, (3948 UE), turns from Bridge Foot into Warwick Road on its way round to the bus station entrance that was just beyond the Red Lion public house. By 6 August 1969, this single-decker was nine years old and looked as if it would continue in service well into the 1970s. Unfortunately, this prospect was rudely altered when Midland Red absorbed the whole Stratford Blue fleet on 1 January 1971. (D.J.Little)

3. 18, (2768 NX)

Peter Sculley, the General Manager who had replaced the late Mr Agg, who had died 'in harness' after twenty-seven years in the job, had a much more of a 'big fleet/ big bus' philosophy about the small Stratford Blue fleet. In 1960 they purchased what proved to be the first of fifteen 30' long Leyland "Titan"PD3s. In later years, Peter Sculley, after leaving Stratford Blue in December 1962, became GM at Aldershot & District and like his former associates at Midland Red, became very active in resisting the formation of the National Bus Company.

18, (2768 NX), waits in the Red Lion bus station in about 1962. It was the middle one of a trio of air-braked, synchromesh gearbox PD3/4s. They were fitted with Willowbrook H41/32F bodies, (yes, a 73 seater!), which at the time was the largest seating capacity of any double-decker in the West Midlands.

The design of these bodies built by the Loughborough company, was one of their better-looking double-decks, being especially tidy around the front of the upper deck. The bus still retains the old-style STRATFORD BLUE fleetname. (R.F.Mack)

4. 18, (2768 NX)

The same bus again, 18, but now numbered 29, (2768 NX), is viewed from the off-side, loads up at the bus station before leaving for Evesham on 6 August 1969. By this time the original opening windscreen had been replaced by a fixed pane which rather spoilt the appearance of the front of the bus. (D.J.Little)

5. 58, (3958 UE)

An unusual purchase by any member of the B.E.T. group was a Ford chassis. Ford Motors started to make inroads into Bedford's domination of the lightweight coach market in 1960 when they introduced their Ford "Thames Trader" 570E chassis. The new Ford chassis was equipped with either a Ford 4.89 litre petrol-engine or a Ford 5.42 litre Diesel engine. It competed directly with the Bedfords SB chassis range. The SB1 had a 4.9 litre oil-engine while the SB3 had the same sized petrol engine. The idiosyncratic Commer "Avenger" IV had Commer's own three-cylinder, horizontally-opposed, supercharged two-stroke 3.26 litre Diesel engine, but sales for the marque were falling dramatically

about this time after the sales onslaught by Bedfords, who were the market leader.

Stratford Blue's solitary Ford 570E was their 58, (3958 UE), which had a Duple "Yeoman" C41F body which had extra cantrail and front dome glasses. It is seen in Victoria Coach Station in about 1962. (A.S.Bronn)

6. 38, (538 EUE)

In January 1963, another four Leyland "Titan" PD3/4s were delivered, but this time the body order was placed with another body manufacturer. 38, (538 EUE), with its Northern Counties H41/32F body, passes through St Giles in the centre of Oxford as it makes its way towards the bus station in about 1969.

These attractive-looking buses were similar in layout to the previous NX-registered PD3/4s delivered three years earlier, though perhaps the typical Northern Counties upper saloon windows gave the vehicles a slightly worried 'frown'. The bus is carrying an poster for a stronger tipple than the more usual Flowers beer advertisements. (R.H.G.Simpson)

7. 59, (8222 NX)

As if to complement the purchase of the Ford 570E, a Bedford SB3, with a similar Duple "Vega" C41F body was acquired in 1962 when the Warwickshire County Garage of Stratford was taken over. Three vehicles, all Bedfords, were involved, but only the newest one, 8222 NX, was taken into the Stratford Blue fleet. It was numbered 59, but it only stayed until the end of the 1963 season of excursions and private hire.

It is seen in London on an excursion, in company with a Leyland belonging to Southdown Motor Services. (R.F.Mack)

8. 50, (5450 WD)

The deep side panels on 50, (5450 WD), reveals that this is one of the Marshall DP41F bodied Leyland "Tiger Cub" PSUC1/1s built in 1962. It is seen when brand new on 19 April 1962 while waiting at the back of the Red Lion bus station in Stratford.

By 1962, the days of the 30' long single-decker were drawing to a close as since July 1961, 36' long, (11 m) single-deckers had been allowed. This marked the beginning of the end of Leyland's "Tiger Cub" range, which gradually was replaced by the longer and larger-engined "Leopard" range, although it took eight more years to disappear from the order books. The rather plain body style, with its flat-front was also soon to disappear. The following year, the B.E.T. Group introduced a much larger, curved windscreen; ironically, because Stratford Blue's flat-fronted "Tiger Cubs" were fairly new, these new B.E.T.-style single-deckers, the norm elsewhere in the country, became a rare type in the Stratford Blue fleet. (J.Cockshot)

9. 55, (5455 WD)

The last of the Marshall-bodied "Tiger Cubs" of 1962 was originally numbered 55, to match its registration number 5455 WD. It was renumbered 53 within a few years, to bring it numerically into the rest of the batch. 55 had a seating capacity of only 41 dual-purpose seating. As a result it could be used on private hire and excursion work to augment the coach fleet. It could be easily distinguished from the rest of the class by the then fashionable aluminium strips around the front half of the vehicle at waistrail level.(R.H.G.Simpson)

10. 16, (JUE 353)

The odd PS2/1 rebuild, in every sense of the word, was the prototype body built on JUE 353 in August 1961. This was bodied by Charles Roe of Crossgates, Leeds with an H35/28F layout. Roe bodies were well-known for their aesthetic qualities, but they did build a number of bodies on metal rather then their traditional teak-frames.

The result was a disaster! The body used Park Royal parts, which appear to have been designed for the A.E.C. "Bridgemaster". The body constructed on JUE 353 had large, deep lower saloon windows, coupled to small depth upper saloon windows with a high sill level. The result was an extremely top heavy design. Not surprisingly, Stratford Blue only had this solitary example.

16 has left the Stratford Blue garage and has entered the Red Lion bus station having crossed Warwick Road. (L.Mason)

11. 33, (JUE 349)

By the early 1960s, the Leyland "Tiger" PS2/3s were becoming 'time-expired' as half-cab single-deckers, though the chassis had plenty of life left in them.

In 1963, four of the chassis were dispatched to Northern Counties of Wigan and were fitted with double-deck bodies. These were 27' long versions of the EUE-registered PD3/4s but because of their length, they had the smaller H35/28F seating capacity.

33, (JUE 349), formerly single-decker 51, had a working life as a double-decker of nine years with Stratford Blue before being sold to G & G Coaches in Leamington, where paradoxically they were often used to work on the former Stratford Blue route to Coventry.

After withdrawal and a number of years of storage, it was beautifully restored into Stratford Blue livery in 1987. It was unfortunately vandalised within two years and was re-rescued for further preservation by B.a M.M.O.T in May 1996. It is seen at the Outer Circle Rally in Birmingham in 1988. (D.R.Harvey)

12. 4, (671 HNX)

The influx of six new PD3 double-deckers continued in 1964 as part of the fleet replacement policy. They replaced the JUE-registered PD2/1s. The six were numbered 1-6 and broke away from the previous ordering policy by being the PD3A/1 model. This model had the St Helens glass-fibre concealed radiator and bonnet assembly, which was better for the bus driver's view from the cab but did nothing for the view of the bus! The body order reverted to Willowbrook and were similar to those supplied with the NX-registered batch of buses.

4, (671 HNX), stands in Oxford Bus Station, in about 1968, in company with a Reliant 'Robin' three-wheeler 'Del Boy' van. (D.R.Harvey Collection)

13. 60, (CWD 33C) / 55, (5455 WD)

Stratford Blue's only standard-looking B.E.T.-bodied vehicle of the mid-1960s was 60, (CWD 33C). This was a 36' Leyland "Leopard" PSU3/3R and had a synchromesh gearbox and air-brakes. It was bodied by Weymann with a B53F seating layout and was fitted with the large front windscreen and rear saloon windows which had been specified by the B.E.T. Group since 1964. 60 was the first Stratford Blue bus, as opposed to coach, delivered in a predominantly white livery. After a few years it was renumbered 54.

Standing next to it in Stratford's bus station is 55, (5455 WD), the Marshall-bodied dual-purpose "Tiger Cub". (D.R.Harvey Collection)

14. 54, (CWD 33C)

How the mighty have fallen! By now numbered 2054 in the Midland Red fleet, CWD 33C waits at the Red Lion bus station when scheduled to work on the 519 service to Shipston-on-Stour.

The bus has been painted into the all-over red livery adopted by Midland Red immediately prior to the compulsory repainting of the fleet into the corporate National Bus Company red. It undoubtedly looked better in the distinctive blue and white livery of its original owners. (A.J.Douglas)

21. 59, (HAC 628D)

In 1966, another solitary single-decker was purchased. This was 62, (HAC 628D) and it was again a Leyland. What made this vehicle unusual was that it was a 30' long "Leopard" but it was the last of the L2 version that was ever constructed. The bus was fitted with an Eaton Two-Speed back axle which effectively meant that it had eight forward gears. 62 was bodied by Marshalls of Cambridge with a DP41F seating configuration and was fitted with forced ventilation, rendering the need for opening saloon ventilators unnecessary. It was renumbered 59 and it was with two thousand added to this new fleet number that it survived with Midland Red until withdrawal in May 1978. It was converted to a yellow-liveried, dual-control driver trainer, latterly based at Worcester.

It is in Banbury bus station in company with 4748, (748 BHA), one of the last D7s to be built and 5905, (PHA 505G), a dual-purpose forty-five seater B.M.M.O. S22 built in 1968 and by sheer coincidence also preserved. (R.F. Mack)

22. 35, (XNX 136H)

The last new vehicle to actually enter service with Stratford Blue was 36, (XNX 136H). This was another Leyland "Leopard", but this time it was a PSU3A/4R type which had a pneumo cyclic gearbox, making life a lot easier for the driver! It was fitted with an Alexander 'Y'-type C49F body, but it was destined to have a short life with Stratford Blue. It was transferred to Midland Red on 1 January 1971, eventually being converted to O.M.O in July 1977. 36 was finally withdrawn in December 1982 by Midland Red North and spent three years being used by a Telford scout group before being sold for preservation in 1985. It is seen after preservation, restored to its original condition. (D.R. Harvey Collection)

23. 33, (AUE 311J) /35, (AUE 313J)

Five Leyland "Panther" PSUR1A/1s were delivered to Stratford Blue in October 1970 as their 31-35, registered XNX 131-135H. the buses were fitted with the rare Marshall "Camair" B41D body with high standee-type nearside windows. They never entered service and were then transferred to Midland Red on that company's absorption of Stratford Blue. They were repainted in all-over red and were re-registered AUE 309-313J. They are in this condition when in store in Adderley Street yard, Deritend, Birmingham keeping company with some unidentifiable B.M.M.O. C3 coach which had been rebodied by Plaxton in 1962.

Midland Red did not use them either. There were industrial relations problems with the crews, though in truth, the reputation of the "Panther" must have been an influence. They were sold to Preston Corporation entering service in their third livery in November 1971. (R.Marshall)

Stratford Blue Tree-Loppers

One of the big problems of any predominantly rural operator is the clearance beneath the trees on the bus routes. The need for tree-loppers for the Stratford Blue Motors was unnecessary until after the purchase of the first batch of Leyland "Titan" PD2/1s in March 1948. Stratford Blue always referred to these conversions as 'Tree-Cutters', hence the TC prefix to the fleet number, though they were used in the main for tree lopping duties.

Stratford Blue's first tree lopper was DB 5166, (seen in the pre-war bus section as a tree-lopper on page 29), which had formerly been numbered 21 in the bus fleet. This tree-lopper was converted in January 1944, presumably to cater for the problems incurred after running the ex-City of Oxford A.E.C."Regent" for four years with increasing amounts of front dome damage. It remained in service in this capacity until January 1952 when it was replaced by TC1.

1. TC1, (DB 9380)

This was the former bus 29 and was registered DB 9380. The Tilling-Stevens B10A2 was converted to a tree-cutter in January 1952 as TC1. It was surprising that the company did not use their Trade Plates on this infrequently used vehicle. The rear of the E.C.O.C. body was converted into an open lorry, while the first three-bays were retained and used for storing recovery and tree-cutting tools. On the roof of the remaining part of the saloon body was a wooden platform. This was used for gaining access to any overhanging branches and foliage, though the garage staff who drew 'the short straw' for doing this work, had little safety features to help them; there wasn't even a rail around the platform. One has to wonder if the vehicle carried a warning sign such as "Tree-cutting without the aid of a safety net!" (D.R.Harvey Collection)

2. TC1, (DHA 731)

The second tree-cutter remained in service until 1955 when it was replaced by a vehicle purchased specially for the task. Stratford Blue had only owned one ex-Midland Red S.O.S.-type vehicle and hired another, so the purchase of DHA 731 was unusual. This had been B.M.M.O. 2113 and was an early type of S.O.S. SON, which was the last model of half-cab single-decker built at Carlyle Road works in Edgbaston. 2113 entered service in 1938 with an English Electric B38F body and was sold out of service in 1955 whereupon Midland Red converted it to its new role, as the new TC1, on behalf of the Stratford Blue company.

TC1 is parked in the garage yard in Stratford in March 1956 when

there was still snow on the ground. Stratford Blue also owned a commercial petrol station at Bridgetown and occasionally the tree-lopper was parked at that site. It was also from this garage that Stratford Blue's car hire service was based, using for many years limousines such as Humber "Pullmans". One of these limousines is parked in front of the tree-lopper. The conversion of TC1 was basically the same as the previous tree-lopper, but if a tree-lopper could be 'luxurious', then this was it! After it was taken out of service in about 1962 TC1 for many years became one of the star attractions at that repository for everything derelict - Bird's scrapyard. (P.Tizard)

Stratford Blue - around the routes

Banbury

2. 43, (GUE 249) /44, (GUE 250)

A pair of Leyland "Tiger" PS1s, 43, (GUE 249) and 44, (GUE 250), load up with passengers in Banbury. At this time, while Midland Red operated the town services out of the bus station in the railway station yard, Stratford Blue buses terminated in North Bar alongside the main A423 just north of the famous Banbury Cross.

The two buses are going back to Kineton via Edgehill. By the mid-1950s, the PS2s were being repainted; 43 has been treated and lost the gold-lining-out while 44 still retains the original, more attractive livery with a white painted waistrail. (D.R.Harvey Collection)

1. 17, (WX 2141)

Resting in the open space in front of the Cock Inn in North Bar near Banbury Cross is Stratford Blue 17, (WX 2141). This was formerly West Yorkshire Road Car 285 and had been purchased in October 1938. It is seen on a summers day just after the end of the Second World War.

The long journeys operated by Stratford Blue to Banbury required these aged buses to climb hills such as Edge Hill or Sun Rising Hill. These exertions are seen with extra cooling for the Tilling-Steven's petrol-engine being supplied by the removal of the bonnet side.

The Roe-bodied Tillings looked a little less dated than the other Tilling or United-bodied examples which were also bought at the same time. (R.H.G.Simpson)

3. 50, (JUE 348)

Crammed into the bus loading point in front of the Georgian Cock Horse public house in North Bar is 50, (JUE 348), in about 1960. The dual-purpose Willowbrook body has lost its white livery-swoop, though the mouldings were retained. It is sandwiched between an elderly Duple-bodied Bedford SB and a late 1950s bus-bodied Bedford SB. To the rear is an operator who had purchased a Beadle-rebuild using pre-war chassis parts.

The Leyland PS2s of Stratford Blue had an active life in their single-decker guise of about twelve

years and were particularly useful when climbing over the Cotswold escarpment from the Avon Valley on the routes to Banbury. (R.Marshall)

4. 48, (3948 UE)

By August 1962, the PS2s had been largely replaced by underfloor-engined single-deckers. Advertising itself as a One-Man-Bus, 48, (3948 UE), a Park Royal-bodied Leyland "Tiger Cub" waits in the North Bar loading area. It is on the route from Banbury to Avon Dassett, a journey which would take about twenty-five minutes.

Even in the days before mass car ownership, the parking area near the Cock Inn was restricted to "Public Service Vehicles and Heavy Lorries Only". (M.A.Sutcliffe)

Birmingham: Around the Bull Ring

1. 39, (GUE 245)

A virtually brand new 39, (GUE 245), a 1948 Leyland "Titan" PD2/1 with a Leyland H30/26R body is parked alongside St Martins Parish church in St Martins Lane, with Spiceal Street behind the bus. In 1948, there was no joint service with Midland Red to Stratford-upon-Avon and it can only be assumed that 39 was on hire to the parent company.

This area of Birmingham was and still is, the main wholesale market area of the city. The Austin K2 lorry of Henry Jones is being unloaded with heedless regard to its obstruction of St Martins Lane and the waiting Great Western Railway lorry. (R.A.Mills)

2. 27, (JUE 355)

A day out 'on the bus' from Birmingham in the 1950s, might be to Tamworth, on the River Tame, to the north, to any of the river towns on the Severn, to Warwick, with its splendid castle or by Stratford Blue bus to Stratford.

The first blue and white buses got into Birmingham on Saturday 31 May 1952, working on the joint 150 service with Midland Red. Judging by the length of the queue, the service was a great success. 27, (JUE 355), one of the 1950 batch of Leyland-bodied PD2/1s stands in front of St Martins church in the Bull Ring waiting for the rush of passengers eagerly anticipating their day out. (M.Rooum)

3. 25, (MAC 572)

As a Ford Model C Ten climbs the Bull Ring, Stratford Blue's 'pride of the fleet', 25, (MAC 572), waits at Stand 3 on the cobbles in front of St Martins church.

The driver and conductor of the bus stand in front of their charge having their half hour break. To the right was a tea bar for the exclusive use of the bus crews, though toilet facilities in the Bull Ring were to say the least minimal!

The bus was still in its first year of service as the Corporation tram overhead was still in place, enabling the trams to reach the overhaul works at Kyotts Lake Road. (M.Rooum)

4. 31, (JUE 359)

The clock on the Victorian tower built in 1855, of St Martins Parish church shows 6:10 p.m., as 31, (JUE 359), turns into Moor Street. A temporary terminus was set up in Moor Street opposite the old G.W.R. railway station. This occurred in 1960, when the rebuilding of the Bull Ring, whose excavations are behind the wooden-stake fencing to the rear of the bus, prevented the original terminus from continuing in use.

The Stratford Blue bus is working into Birmingham before leaving on the company's last journey of the day back to Stratford; evening journeys were worked by Midland Red. Behind the double-decker, climbing up the Bull Ring is an elderly Perkins Diesel-engined Bedford OB coach with a Willowbrook body relegated to being a contractors bus. (R.F.Mack)

5. 28, (JUE 356)

Buses journeying to Stratford-upon-Avon on the 150 service frequently stopped in Spiceal Street alongside St Martins church, around the corner from the main bus stop.

28, (JUE 356), has been parked, or abandoned judging by its distance from the kerb, in Spiceal Street opposite a 1957 Vauxhall Cresta six-cylinder car. The shops alongside the car, including Timpsons the shoe shop, were swept away in 1961 as part of the 'redevelopment' of the Bull Ring area. The rabbit-warren of alleyways, narrow streets and interesting shops and buildings were replaced with the Bull Ring Centre which although always something of a white elephant, was Britain's first indoor shopping centre. (D.R.Harvey Collection)

6. 23, (MAC 570), / 4497, XHA 497)

When the demand for buses to Stratford was heavy, Midland Red inspectors would send the buses from their usual stands in front of St Martins, down the hill into Spiceal Street and sometimes even beyond that, into Jamaica Row.

One of the trio of Leyland-bodied Leyland PD2/12s, waits alongside Smithfield fruit and vegetable market which had been built in 1881. 23, (MAC 570), stands in front of Midland Red B.M.M.O. D7, 4497, (XHA 497). The Midland Red single-deckers in the background are parked where 28, (JUE 356), was parked in the previous photograph.

So how did the passengers know where their bus to Stratford was parked? The same inspectors

simply sent the passengers on a three hundred yard march to the buses - hopefully not to see their intended bus disappearing! (R.F.Mack)

7. 21, (TNX 455)

The crew of Willowbrook-bodied Leyland "Titan" PD2/12, 21, (TNX 455), enjoy a quiet smoke while standing next to Smithfield Market in Jamaica Row. Passengers are already sitting upstairs while another person has trooped down the hill from the Bull Ring in order to catch the bus. Parked behind 21 is a Morris-Commercial PV van, which appears to be missing its off-side headlight. (A.J.Douglas)

8. 35, (JUE 351)

The 'temporary' bus terminus in Moor Street survived long enough to see the completion of the Bull Ring Shopping Centre. It is in the background behind the statue of Lord Nelson, which, in 1809 was the first memorial built in the country to the late Admiral and his posthumous victory at Trafalgar.

On 1 November 1963, the new Birmingham Bus Station in Edgbaston Street was opened as part of the first phase of the Bull Ring Centre. The Coventry Road, Stratford Road and Warwick Road services operated by

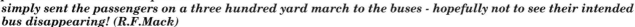

Midland Red and Stratford Blue were all moved in to the new bus station from Moor Street. The presence of any of the 1963 Northern Counties rebodied Leyland "Tiger" PS2/3, in this case 35, (JUE 351), is therefore quite unusual as they were only in service for a few months before all these services were moved into the new bus station. (L.Mason)

9. 19, (2769 NX)

Leyland "Titan" PD3/4, 19, (2769 NX), fitted with a Willowbrook H41/32F body, descends the Bull Ring surrounded by trafic. A Ford 300E 5 cwt van and an Austin A35 van are both overtaking the bus, while in Park Street, beyond the multi-storey car park is a Jowett "Javelin" and an Austin A40 "Somerset". Behind these two cars is the Royal George public house which was replaced by a new building of the same name in 1964. (L.Mason)

Bull Ring Bus Station

1. 5, (672 HNX)

Willowbrook-bodied Leyland "Titan" PD3A/1, formerly Stratford Blue 5, (672 HNX), repainted in Midland Red livery and renumbered 2005, has arrived at the entrance to the Bull Ring bus station in 1971. It is about to turn from Dudley Street into the bus station in a manoeuvre that would be impossible today as the traffic flow has been reversed. This bus would only stay with Midland Red until May 1972 when it would be sold to Isle of Man Road Services as their number 65. These double-deckers were the first in the fleet to have the large one-piece destination box, rather than the earlier separate boxes and this new design gave the vehicles a more modern appearance, though it did nothing for the legibility of the display! (D.R.Harvey Collection)

2. 7, (GUE 1D)

The stygian gloom of the Birmingham Bus Station in the subterranean depths of the Bull Ring Shopping Centre was held as a breakthrough when it was opened in November 1963. Unfortunately, this euphoria was quickly to be choked by the build-up of exhaust fumes and poor access. By the late 1980s many operators had reverted to loading up again in the congested city streets before many of the streets succumbed to being pedestrianised a decade later.

Stratford Blue 7, (GUE 1D), waits at its loading point in the bus station, it's driver having employed the normal practice of switching on the saloon lights so that passengers could see their way onto the bus. It is about 1968 and the bus is about to work the 150 service back to its home town. (L.Mason)

3. 8, (GUE 2D)

The last of the Leyland "Titan" PD3A/1s bought by Stratford Blue in 1966 was 8, (GUE 2D). It has just left the Bull Ring Bus Station and is at the Edgbaston Street - Pershore Street junction when setting out on its 23 mile journey back to Stratford-upon-Avon. It is being followed by one of Sutton Coldfield garage's B.M.M.O. D9s, 4858, (858 KHA), registered in 1960, which is working on the 111 service to Roughley. (D.Williams)

The Prestigious 150 Route
Birmingham - Henley-in-Arden - Stratford

1. 22, (TNX 456)

The 150 service, being a Stage Carriage route, loaded up either outside St Martins Parish church in the Bull Ring or latterly in the Birmingham Bull Ring Bus Station. Some of Midland Red's famous 'X' express routes passing through Birmingham actually went into Digbeth Coach Station, but the 150 service was never granted this privilege.

Leyland "Titan" PD2/12, 22, (TNX 456), passes the coach station on its way into the city centre in about 1963. It was one of the three Willowbrook-bodied sixty-three seaters built in 1956 and is being followed through Digbeth by one of the reverse-rear window Ford "Anglia" 105Es. (A.J.Douglas)

2. 29, (JUE 357)

On its way out of the city to Stratford-upon-Avon, the 150 service travelled through Birmingham's Digbeth, Deritend and Camp Hill areas before arriving at the "gate-way-like" Camp Hill railway bridge. This marked the beginning of Stratford Road, which until the opening of the M40 motorway, was the main A34 route to Stratford and Oxford and beyond to Newbury and Winchester.

29, (JUE 357), was one of the second batch of Leyland "Titan" PD2/1s with Leyland H30/26R bodies, passes through the 16' arch of the former Midland Railway's bridge, which had been built by the Birmingham and Gloucester Railway in 1841. The destination of the Stratford Blue

bus carried the legend 'ON HIRE TO MIDLAND RED' as the route was licensed to Midland Red. This meant that Stratford Blue had to charge Midland Red fares on the service. In the distance, a Midland Red Leyland "Titan" PD2/12, LD8-type is travelling into the city. This scene has hardly changed in the intervening years since 1960 when JUE 357 passed through the bridge with the Austin A35 car travelling in the opposite direction, though where the LD8 is waiting is now part of Birmingham's Middle Ring Road. (R.Marshall)

3. 32, (JUE 348)

On a murky morning, 32, (JUE 348), one of the Northern Counties rebodied Leyland "Tiger" PS2/1s emerges from the gloom. It is passing through the School Road traffic lights at the Horse Shoe public house in the Hall Green section of Stratford Road as it travels into Birmingham on the 150 service.

The rebodying of these single-deckers in 1963 gave Stratford Blue a batch of very useful double-deckers. Being 27' 6" long, they had sixty-three seats, which effectively gave the company an extra seven seats over the GUE-batch of Leyland PD2/1s which were being withdrawn that year. (L.Mason)

4. 5, (672 HNX)

Once beyond the Birmingham city boundary at Hall Green, the 150 service reached Shirley. Shirley is part of Solihull and had been developed in the 1930s as a shopping centre along the main Stratford Road to serve the western side of Solihull. It had the advantage of being on the main A34 and as a result became a useful source of income on the Birmingham-Stratford service. Leyland "Titan" PD3A/1, 672 HNX, by now painted in Midland Red colours and renumbered 2005, travels towards Stratford on a 150 service, having passed the Bull's Head public house in the background and one of the first Chinese restaurants in the region, aptly named "Shirley Temple"! (L.Mason)

5. 3, (670 HNX)

While the repainting of the Stratford Blue buses into Midland Red's colours was very striking, somehow the buses lost their individuality when the smart blue and white livery was replaced. Leyland "Titan" PD3A/1, 3,(670 HNX), renumbered 2003 by Midland Red, has just entered Henley-in-Arden High Street at the north end of the village and is passing the Black Swan public house in the spring of 1971.

Henley-in-Arden is situated about two-thirds of the way between Birmingham and Stratford. Until the 1960's, when commuting to Birmingham by car began to develop, Henley-in-Arden had very few buildings lying away from the High Street. Most of the thoroughfare was lined by picturesque Elizabethan, Jacobean and Georgian buildings and this unspoilt linear layout made this large village almost unique in the West Midlands. (R.H.G.Simpson)

6. 23, (MAC 570)

For most people, Henley-in-Arden was most famous for its Tudor Dairy's ice creams, for which, on hot summer days, most bus passengers and even passing motorists 'would die' for one of their '99's!

When first delivered, the three MAC-registered Leyland-bodied "Titan" PD2/12s had open rear platforms; doors were fitted retrospectively. The first of the trio, 23, MAC 570), waits in Henley High Street by the Three Tuns pub, when in this unenclosed state, beyond the 15th Century church of St John the Baptist. The clock on the tower shows 1:35 p.m., suggesting that the bus is either half an hour late or that the clock is broken! Behind the bus is a Morris Eight saloon dating from about 1935. (R.H.G.Simpson)

7. 25, (MAC 572)

No doubt giving its many passengers the benefit of its top speed, 25, (MAC 572), speeds down the hill from Wootten Wowen towards Henley-in-Arden on the 150 service. By this time the company had fitted the excellent 'Farington'-styled Leyland bodies with platform doors. The taper at the front end of the bodied shows how Leyland designers had adapted the 7' 6" wide body into a new 8' wide structure by using the minimum number of new components and getting away with it! (A.J.Douglas)

Cheltenham Spa

1. 33, (GUE 239)

Stratford Blue Leyland "Titan" PD2/1, 33, (GUE 239), has arrived in Cheltenham Bus Station working on the 64A service from Evesham,, It is a Saturday afternoon in August 1958 and the bus is by this date painted in the newly introduced simplified livery which omitted the gold lining-out. Behind the Stratford Blue bus is a normal-control Leyland "Comet" CPO1 with a Harrington coach body.

The bus station, off Royal Well, was overlooked by the very Regency buildings which so characterised the town. On the other side of the bus shelters the terrace was occupied by Cheltenham's council offices. (D.Wootton)

2. 31, (JUE 359)

A few years earlier in 1951, 31, (JUE 359), has begun to load up with passengers in Cheltenham Bus Station. Unlike 33 in the previous photograph, the driver of JUE 359 has turned the destination blind back to show 64A EVESHAM before embarking on the just over one hour journey.

In both Evesham and Cheltenham, Stratford Blue came into contact with buses owned by the Bristol Omnibus Company. Parked behind the PD2/1 is 3707, (KHY390), a 1948 Bristol K5G with an E.C.W. H30/26R body. It is working on the 62 service that will take the bus further north along the Severn Valley to Tewkesbury.

Cheltenham's bus station was opened in the1930s and with its concrete bus shelters, was quite an advanced piece of urban planning. It was both central to the town and yet allowed good access for buses. A measure of its success is that it has hardly changed over the intervening years. (D.R.Harvey Collection)

3. 18, (2768 NX)

On a wet afternoon, a Willowbrook-bodied forward-entrance Leyland "Titan" PD3/4, 18, (2768 NX), leaves Cheltenham Bus Station on the 64A service to Evesham. The one hour ten minute journey would take the bus through a succession of small villages such as Teddington Hands and Dumbleton.

Behind the bus in the distance is the tree-lined turning circle in which is standing a Burlingham bodied half-cab coach dating from the end of the 1940s. To the left of the Stratford Blue bus are the Regency terraces which line Royal Crescent. (A.J.Douglas)

4. 51, (5451 WD)

By the mid-1960s, financial considerations caused by the reduction of passengers and the increase in car ownership, meant that single-deckers were more and more frequently employed on the Evesham to Cheltenham 64A service. Further economies were also made when many of the off-peak journeys were operated by a fare-collecting driver.

Parked in the shade, beneath the trees in the turning loop of Cheltenham Bus Station is Marshall-bodied, Leyland "Tiger Cub" PSUC1/1, 51, (5451 WD), which had entered service in 1961. Despite having only bus seats, the deep cushions would be comfortable enough for most long journeys. It was only to remain in service for ten years as it was one of the first tranche of Stratford Blue withdrawals after the Midland Red takeover, going in April 1971. (A.D.Broughall)

5. 49, (5449 WD)

Passing through the Regency streets of Cheltenham is another of the Marshall-bodied Leyland "Tiger Cubs". 49, (5449 WD), by now repainted in the later simplified livery of the mid-1960s, has come into Cheltenham Spa by way of the Evesham Road when working on the 64A service. The driver of the bus is breaking 'the rules', even on a warm day, by driving the One-Man-Operated single-decker with its power doors wide open. (A.J.Douglas)

Cheltenham Spa Coach Station

1. 53, (JUE 351)

Cheltenham's famous coach station in St Margaret's Road was originally opened in 1932. It remained as an important hub of the Associated Motorways Group's operations until motorways services became more accessible for coaches.

Towards the end of its single-decker career, about 1959, Stratford Blue's 53, (JUE 351), is being used by Associated Motorways as a relief connecting vehicle. Behind 53, suitcased holiday makers wait for their coaches to arrive. These would take them on to holiday destinations served by companys such as Red and White and Black and White, both of whose underfloor engined coaches are alongside or behind the Stratford Blue vehicle. (A.J.Douglas)

2. 43, (2744 AC)

A few years later, in about 1963, Cheltenham Spa's Coach Station had all the same characteristics of regimented line-ups of coaches and intending, worried passengers milling about in search of their coach.

Stratford Blue's policy of purchasing dual-purpose single-deckers was of great value to them. On summer weekends, many of them could be seen being used as feeder vehicles or occasionally as substitute coaches.

43, (2744 AC), the last of the quartet of 1959 Leyland"Tiger Cubs" with Willowbrook DP41F bodies, waits at the exit of the Coach Station looking as if forty-one coach seats might not be sufficient. (A.J.Douglas)

Coventry

1. 24, (MAC 571)

Pool Meadow Bus Station is, in bus terms, usually associated with Coventry Corporation's chocolate and white buses and the all-over red of Midland Red. It is forgotten that Stratford Blue had an occasional presence in the city.

Working on hire to Midland Red on the 517 service between Coventry, Kenilworth and Leamington Spa is 24, (MAC 571). More usually associated with this route were the very similar, but concealed radiatored Midland Red SHA-registered LD8s.

Unlike many city bus stations, the bus shelters in Pool Meadow did offer the intending passenger some protection from inclement weather. Unfortunately, in order to get to the bus station, passengers would have almost certainly got soaked as its position off Fairfax Street is at the very edge of the city and usually meant a long walk!

Parked behind the double-decker is B.M.M.O. S14, 4567, (567 AHA), working on the 538 service to Kenilworth and behind that is a KVC-registered Daimler CVD6 and a Daimler CVA6, both belonging to Coventry Corporation. (A.D.Broughall)

2. 58, (3958 UE)

Stratford Blue's solitary Ford 570E, 58, (3958 UE) stands on the parking area away from the bus stops in Pool Meadow on 24 July 1965. This was the Ford's last year in service and it had lost its front wheel-trims. It is on hire to Midland Red, but apparently isn't doing too much business.

In the background, standing at the bus stops, as well as the Coventry Corporation M.C.C.W. 'Orion'-bodied Daimler CVG6, is a Midland Red SHA-registered LD8 working on the 517 service to Leamington. (P.J.Relf)

Evesham

1. 40, (GUE 246)

The Stratford Blue 5A service to Evesham via Bidford and Cranhill terminated in High Street in front of the Clifton cinema. This view can be dated to 1951, as the film being shown at the picture-house is "The Browning Version". This was based on a Terence Rattigan play and starred Michael Redgrave.

Leyland "Tiger" PS1, 40, (GUE 246), loads up before making the return journey back to Stratford. The attractive Northern Coach Builders B34F body, of which Stratford Blue had ten of the eleven built, bore a remarkable resemblance to the much more common B.E.T. bodies built by Brush. (D.R.Harvey Collection)

2. 55, (JUE 353)

A positively gleaming Leyland "Tiger" PS2/1 55, (JUE 353), one of the pair of Willowbrook bus-bodied single-deckers built in 1950 stands in the bus 'station' in High Street, Evesham, which was between Swan Lane and Oat Street. As was the case in Banbury, the buses used the widened main street of the town as a bus station.

55 is about to leave Evesham when working on the 64A service to Cheltenham. It is about 1957 as the most modern car visible is a Standard 10, parked on the extreme left in company with a Ford 'Anglia' and an Austin 12 saloon of about 1947. (R.Gingell)

3. 28, (JUE 356)

When nearly new, all-Leyland PD2/1 28, (JUE 356), is just about to be boarded by two young girls and their mother. The bus is waiting to work on the 64 service from Evesham to Cheltenham.

The Georgian and Victorian buildings of High Street, Evesham make an attractive backdrop to this scene in which the Stratford Blue bus is the most modern vehicle.

These JUE-registered Leylands had an unusual appearance for standard Leyland bodies. They had opening sliding ventilators in every saloon window, which was rarely specified elsewhere. (D.R.Harvey Collection)

4. 2, (669 HNX)

By the mid-1960s, the PS2 single-deckers and the two batches of Leyland-bodied Leyland PD2s had all been replaced. 2, (669 HNX), one of the first St Helens-style fronted Leyland "Titan" PD3A/1s stands in the bus station alongside High Street in Evesham.

By this time, the use of 30' long double-deckers on the 5 service from Evesham to Stratford via Luddington and Bidford-on-Avon, was fairly normal practice. The only problem with this was that Evesham's bus station, particularly on market days and summer Saturdays, must have become quite a squeeze for these larger double-deckers. (Bristol Vintage Bus Group)

5. 39, (539 EUE)

By now renumbered in the Stratford Blue fleet as their 27, the former 39, (539 EUE), stands at the bus stop on the opposite side of Evesham's High Street to the bus station. It is facing towards Stratford and is about to leave on the 5A service once it had re-acquired its two-man crew.

This bus lay-by outside Evesham's main Post Office was generally only used as a normal bus stop. On this miserable-looking summer Thursday, 8 July 1969, a Ford "Corsair" speeds by while across the road, a Black and White Plaxton-bodied coach appears to be parked illegally half-on and half-off the pavement. (D.J.Little)

Kineton

1. 32, (GUE 238)

Followed by a four-wheeled Berkeley sports car, Stratford Blue's first post-war bus, 32, (GUE 238), comes into Kineton on the B4086 from Stratford, despite its destination blind. It is making its way back to Stratford Blue's garage in Kineton and is about to pass the junction with Bridge Street opposite the church. The bus, in Church Mews, has behind it the Kineton Public Hall built in 1894. The lack of traffic in about 1960 is quite remarkable as the spotless Leyland, by now in the more simplified livery, takes a fairly leisurely run back to base. These early GUE-registered double-deckers boasted the impressive large headlights which were standard in the early post-war years and which had been inherited from the previous "Titan" PD1 model. (A.J.Douglas)

2. 46, (GUE 252)

On a warm summers day in Kineton, Leyland "Tiger" PS1 46, (GUE 252), has its conductor issuing his tickets on the pavement. The bus is about to go on the comparatively short journey of three miles to Wellesbourne. It is parked on the B4086 road to Stratford near to Bridge Street and opposite St Peters Church, a lovely toffee coloured sandstone church, whose tower dates from the late thirteenth century. (J.H. Taylforth)

Royal Leamington Spa

1. 22, (TNX 456)

The Leamington terminus for Stratford Blue was in Old Warwick Road outside the former Great Western Railway station. Buses used to park-up in lay-over periods on the opposite side of the road in the yard next to Midland Red's Leamington garage. It is here that 22, (TNX 456), one of the Leyland "Titan" PD2/12s with a Willowbrook H35/28R body is parked. (D.R.Harvey Collection)

2. 34, (GUE 240)

Waiting to load up outside Leamington Spa railway station, with its windows steamed up, is 34, (GUE 240), a Leyland "Titan" PD2/1. Just for once, the inclement weather has rather spoilt the normally immaculate appearance of this Stratford Blue double-decker.

Royal Leamington Spa gained the prefix 'Royal' and suffix 'Spa' after Queen Victoria visited the spa baths in 1838. The restorative properties of the waters led to the rapid growth of the town between 1820 and 1840 with some quite glorious Regency terraces and crescent. The Great Western Railway arrived in the town in 1844 and with it, on the south side of the River Leam, a typical set of their simply-styled station buildings. (P.Trevaskis)

3. 44, (2745 AC)

The underfloor-engined Leyland "Tiger Cubs" were quickly employed as Pay-As-You-Enter, One-Man-Operated buses, especially on the more rural routes.

44, (2745 AC), a Willowbrook B45F bodied example of 1959, waits in Old Warwick Road outside Leamington's railway station in company with Midland Red S14, 4346, (UHA 346), a bus which was three years older than the Stratford Blue bus. 44 is working on the 33 route to Moreton Paddox in about 1964 and is well loaded with passengers waiting to start their half-hour journey. (R.F.Mack)

4. 1, (668 HNX)

As an English Electric Type 4 1Co-Co1 Diesel-Electric locomotive waits to take its train southwards out of Leamington Spa railway station, Leyland "Titan" PD3A/1, 1, (668 HNX), stands at the bus terminus in Old Warwick Road.

The bus is working on the 32A service to Kineton via Gaydon. This route was well-patronised by R.A.F. personnel from the famous 'V' jet-bomber base at Gaydon, going on and returning from leave. (A.J.Douglas)

5. 45, (GUE 251)

Leyland "Tiger" PS1, 45, (GUE 251), lies over beneath the railway arches in Lower Avenue outside Beasley's Stores. The Northern Coach Builders bodied single-decker is working on the Marlborough Farm Central Armaments Depot service in the mid-1950s. This service only ran to the C.A.D. when the camp required buses. The Leyland is still in its original lined-out livery. (P.Trevaskis)

6. 24, (536 EUE)

Leyland "Titan" PD3/4 24, (536 EUE), with a Northern Counties body, returns to Leamington's bus station after working on the 90A service on a journey from Stratford, Snitterfield and Warwick that was timetabled at fifty minutes. The bus station was behind Leamington Spa's railway stations off Spencer Street occupying land next to the River Leam. (F.York)

London - Victoria Coach Station

1. 56, (OUE 11)

Stratford Blue's coach fleet was regularly used to augment Midland Red's coaches on both private hire duties and on the regular coach services operated by the parent company.

56, (OUE 11), the first of the pair of Leyland "Royal Tiger" PSU1/16s with an attractive Burlingham "Seagull" body, is parked in a damp Victoria Coach Station in the West End of London. It is parked with two of Aldershot & District's Strachan-bodied A.E.C. "Reliances" of 1954.

In these pre-motorway days, the journey back to the Midlands would be via Edgware Road and the A41 and was timed at five and a half hours. (R.Marshall)

2. 40, (2741 AC)

In company with the Standerwick 'Gay Hostess' Leyland "Atlantean" double-deck coach, is the much humbler Leyland 'Tiger Cub' of Stratford Blue. It is one of the dual-purpose Willowbrook-bodied vehicles which entered service in 1959.

40, (2741 AC), is parked in the Victoria Coach Station yard, seemingly as usual on hire to Midland Red. Despite their bus outline, these vehicles were quite well suited to medium distance coach-substitute working, such as the long run to London, as they offered quite comfortable seating for their passengers. (D.R.Harvey Collection)

Oxford

1. 7, (GUE 1D)

The 44 route between Stratford-upon-Avon and Oxford was operated by Stratford Blue and City of Oxford Motor Services. There were only four buses each way per day and passengers wanting to go beyond Long Compton had to re-book their tickets.

Leyland "Titan" PD3A/1, 7, (GUE 1D), passes along Oxford Street in Woodstock, having set down some of its passengers outside the Marlborough Arms Hotel in 1967. This hotel is the beautiful Georgian building behind the bus made of the soft ochre-coloured Cotswold Jurassic Limestone. To the right is the clothes shop owned by J.Banbury and Son, which to this day still has the yellow blinds in the window to prevent the displays from fading. (R.H.G. Simpson)

2. 52, (JUE 350)

The four dual-purpose Willowbrook-bodied Leyland "Tiger" PS2/3 were ideally suited for work on the 44 service to Oxford. 52, (JUE 350), has arrived at Gloucester Green Bus Station from Stratford. The service must have been popular as parked behind this bus is another PS2, 54, (JUE 352), only this is one of the bus bodied pair. On the destination blind of 54 is the legend 'RELIEF' suggesting that the Stratford to Oxford service was beginning to need the services of double-deckers.

The single-decker parked on the right belonging to City of Oxford Motor Services is an A.E.C. "Regal" III and is also fitted with a Willowbrook body. (R.H.G. Simpson)

3. 28, (JUE 356)

The buses working on the 44 service between Stratford and Oxford showed the ultimate destination. This was despite the lack of through running on as far as the two operators were concerned and that buses from both operators were found at 'the wrong end of the route' working 'shorts'.

In the early 1950s, Leyland "Titan" PD2/1 28, (JUE 356), lies over in company with two of City of Oxford's A.E.C.s in Oxford's Gloucester Green Bus Station. The use of these Leylands and City of Oxford's A.E.C. "Regent" IIIs must have been a revelation to passengers who for years had suffered the perils of the underpowered Stratford Blue Tilling-Stevens. (R.H.G. Simpson)

4. 21, TNX 455)

In 1958, Stratford Blue 21, (TNX 455), loads up with passengers in Gloucester Green Bus Station although its crew have yet to change the double-deckers destination display back to its correct setting.

Behind the bus is the slightly run-down Corn Exchange Hotel which still dominates the entrance of the present-day bus station.

These Willowbrook-bodied Leyland "Titan PD2/12s were mechanically identical to the MAC-registered Leyland 'Farington'-bodied double-deckers, being powered by the same 9.8 litre Leyland 0.600 engine and also being 27' long.

There the resemblance ended as the four-bay bodies, although attractive enough, did not have the design flair that so characterised the Bailey-inspired Leyland bodies. (J.Cockshot)

5. 3, (670 HNX)

The driver of Stratford Blue 3, (670 HNX), a 1963 30' long Leyland "Titan" PD3A/1 has abandoned his vehicle half way into the loading bay for the 44 service.

The bus is about one year old and behind it is a fascinating collection of cars including on the left a black Morris 'Oxford' and a Ford 'Anglia' E93A representing cars of the early 1950s and a Triumph 'Herald' and a Morris Minivan, exemplifying vehicles of a decade later. (D.R. Harvey Collection)

6. 35, (JUE 351)

Displaying the fleet number 135, which it received in April 1970, JUE 351, a Northern Counties-bodied Leyland "Tiger" PS2/3, is parked well into the middle of Gloucester Green Bus Station. Alongside it is a Marshall-bodied A.E.C. "Reliance" built in 1962 for City of Oxford Motor Services and an older "Reliance" parked behind. Surprisingly, the lay-over at Oxford was timetabled for only ten minutes, before the return journey back to Stratford via Woodstock, Chipping Norton and Shipston-on-Stour was begun. (A.J.Douglas)

7. 11, (NAC 417F)

In the last few years of Stratford Blue operation, the three Northern Counties-bodied Leyland "Atlantean" PDR1A/1s became regular performers on the joint 44 service between Stratford and Oxford. So popular were they that City of Oxford Motor Services bought the three in May 1971. 11, (NAC 417F), is about to leave Gloucester Green Bus Station on its way back to Stratford, about two years before it became Oxford's 906.

Gloucester Green Bus Station is still in use today, but is a far more modern and inviting place than the run down terminus of 1970. (R.H.G.Simpson)

Shipston-On-Stour

1. HIGH STREET c.1920

One of the hidden gems in Warwickshire is the market town of Shipston-on-Stour. This was one of the earliest settlements which was served by Grail and Joiners Stratford Blue Motors. The main road has for many years skirted behind the main street and because of this, the town centre has remained largely unspoilt and unaltered for well over a century.

High Street is lined with some splendid Georgian buildings. High Street is a wide, but deceptively short street being almost closed at the end behind the photographer. In this early 1920s view, the three-storied George Hotel, with its sign overhanging the street, is on the left. Beyond it is another lovely three-storied hotel and it parked in that building's shadow that an unidentified Warwickshire registered single-decker stands. It is not one of Stratford Blue's vehicles, but is included here as it shows one of the smaller towns which Stratford Blue served for virtually the whole of its existence. (Shakespeare Birthplace Library)

Stratford - a journey around the town

1. 50, (5450 WD)

Leyland "Tiger Cub" PSUC1/1/ 50, (5450 WD), one of the five Marshall-bodied single-deckers delivered in 1962, speeds out of Stratford on the A34 Birmingham Road. It is working on the L3 local service to Justins Avenue, having just passed the site of Bird's famous bus scrapyard.

Towering over the early 20th century terraces is the huge Flowers Brewery, part of which dated from 1831. Flowers was one of the main employers in the town until they were taken-over by the giant Whitbread Group. The Flowers family were also great benefactors, financially supporting many schemes in Stratford including the Royal Shakespeare Theatre. Of course, most of the Stratford Blue bus fleet at some time had an advertisement for Flower's beers adorning them. (R.F.Mack)

2. 5, (672 HNX)

Travelling into Stratford on the Birmingham Road at Bird's scrapyard, is 5, (672 HNX), a seventy-three seater Leyland "Titan" PD3A/1 of 1963, which by this time its front destination box had been rebuilt to conform to those on GUE 1D and GUE 2D. It is returning to Bridge Street on the L3 service from Justins Avenue. This scene has changed considerably in the intervening years with the main A34 road being widened and a large out-of-town retail park being opened on the site of the former bus scrapyard. (R.F.Mack)

3. 17, (2767 NX)

The former 17, (2767 NX), now renumbered 28, a PD3/4 with a Willowbrook body, speeds along the recently opened Bridgeway. It is working around the one-way street system in the town back towards the Red Lion bus station in about 1967. It is being followed by a Rover 2000, a Hillman Minx and at the rear, behind the Bedford TK lorry, is an Austin Mini. (R.F.Mack)

4. 19, (2769 NX)

30, (2767 NX), another of the trio of 1960 Leyland "Titan" PD/4s with Willowbrook H41/32F bodies, by now, in the mid-1960s, renumbered 30, enters the Red Lion Bus Station off Warwick Road. As the bus is empty, it has probably just come from the Stratford Blue garage on the corner of Guild Street and Warwick Road. This particular bus had an eleven and a half year career with Stratford Blue after which it ran as Isle of Man Road Services 43 for nearly another eight years. (D.R.Harvey Collection)

5. 54, (JUE 352)

The two bus Willowbrook-bodied Leyland "Tiger" PS2/1 had very similar-looking bodies to the dual-purpose versions. The main external difference was at the rear, where the emergency exit was set in the back panel, resulting in two side windows and a windowed door. The dual-purpose vehicles had their emergency exits in the short off-side front-bay behind the front bulkhead and opposite the main entrance.

54, (JUE 352) painted with a cantrail advertisement for Flowers Ale, stands in the bus station near to the Midland Red booking office in 1950. (S.N.J.White)

6. 32, (JUE 348)

Rebodied Leyland "Tiger" PS2/3 stands between the back of the Red Lion public house and the Midland Red Booking office. It is waiting to take up its next run to the village of Broom, with splendid old inn, on the 5A service on 6 August 1969. By this date, the Red Lion was no longer a Flowers-owned public house as it had been taken-over by Whitbread when the local brewery sold out to the large national brewer. (D.J.Little)

7. 45, (GUE 251)

The Brush-look-alike N.C.B.-bodies on the Leyland PS1s were very attractive looking buses, save for their windscreen treatment. It does appear that the composite body on 45, (GUE 251), is beginning to show signs of wear and tear as the waistrail beading is slightly sagging and some of the panels are beginning to ripple.

The bus waits alongside the route noticeboard at the exit alongside the Red Lion public house when working on the 519 service to Newbold in 1959. (A.J. Douglas)

8. 47, (GUE 253)

All of Stratford Blue's out-of-town services radiated from the Red Lion Bus Station. Here, one summers evening in 1958, parked alongside the Red Lion public house, which like the bus, is advertising Flowers beer, is N.C.B.-bodied Leyland "Tiger" PS1, 47, (GUE 253). Just visible on the right is a Black & White underfloor-engined coach. (D.R.Harvey Collection)

9. 52, (JUE 350)

The location of the departure points in Stratford's bus station seemed to be something of a moveable feast. Buses generally loaded up where there was a space which gave access to the junction of Bridgefoot and Warwick Road. Just to prove that there is an exception to every rule, 52, (JUE 350), waiting to work on the 5A service, is parked next to a wooden noticeboard painted with the destination 'EVESHAM'

Propped-up over the bonnet is a slip-board showing that this dual-purpose-bodied PS2/3 is going via the village of Grafton. (A.B.Cross)

10. 33, (GUE 239) / B.M.M.O. 3052, (HHA 653)

Summer Saturdays at Stratford Bus Station were always scenes of frenetic arrivals and departures as intending passengers milled around the buses looking for their bus.

Stratford Blue's 33, (GUE 239), one of the Leyland-bodied Leyland PD2/1s delivered in 1948, stands next to Midland Red's B.M.M.O. S6, 3052, (HHA 653) in about 1960. This was one of the Metro-Cammell-bodied S6s which differed from the Brush-bodied examples by the outward curves of the front-profile at the bottom of the destination box. The S6, destined to be withdrawn in 1962, is working to Leamington via Wellesbourne on the 518 route.

On the extreme right is an A.E.C."Regent" V of City of Oxford Motor Services, waiting to return to Oxford on the 44 service, while behind the S6 is a Midland Red double-decker. This is a Metro-Cammell-bodied B.M.M.O. D7 which is working on the 150 service to Birmingham.

On the extreme left is another Stratford Blue vehicle, this time a forward-entrance PD3/4, while the roof of another GUE-registered PD2/1 is just visible behind the City of Oxford bus. (A.S. Bronn)

11. 37, (GUE 243) / 26, (JUE 354)

A much quieter day in the bus station has one of each of the two batches of Leyland "Titan" PD2/1s waiting to go on 'local' village services. It affords the opportunity to compare the 1948 Leyland body style with that of one built in 1950.

37, (JUE 243), is waiting to go to Shottery, while 26, (JUE 354), is off on the three mile, fifteen minute trip to Loxley. 26 was the only one of the six 1950 batch of Leyland-bodied PD2/1s not to have every saloon side window fitted with ventilators.(A.D.Broughall)

12. 7, (GUE 1D) / 8, (GUE 2D)

The five year old twins of 1966, 7, (GUE 1D) and 8, (GUE 2D), by now numbered 2007 and 2008 in the Midland Red fleet and painted all-over red, stand at the exit of the Red Lion bus station in 1972.

Within a few months, these modern, reliable buses, would be sold off to the Isle of Man Road services, leaving Stratford for the next few years to the gentle mercies of double-deckers such as the B.M.M.O. D9 parked next to the pair of Leylands. (R.F.Mack)

13. 49, (5449 WD)

49, (5449 WD), turns from Bridge Street by the Anchor public house on its way into Warwick Road as it returns from West Green Drive to the bus station. The bus is one of the attractively-proportioned Marshall dual-purpose Leyland "Tiger Cub" PSUC1/1s of 1962. It is perhaps surprising, however, that the B.E.T. Group was still specifying a flat front with a split recessed driver's windscreen for their single-deckers as late as this date. (D.R.Harvey Collection)

14. 35, (JUE 351)

With the Royal Shakespeare Theatre and the Bancroft Gardens just visible beyond the trees lining Waterside, rebodied PS2/3, 35, (JUE 351), comes into Warwick Road. It has come from Bridge Street and will shortly cross the bottom of Guild Street and pass Stratford Blue's bus garage when working on the local town service L4 from Banbury Road. (D.R.Harvey Collection)

15. 34, (GUE 240)

Before the opening of Bridgeway and the development of the one-way-street system, Stratford's through traffic along the A34, came out of Guild Street, into Bridgefoot, passing the bus station on the left and the Unicorn public house before crossing the River Avon on the medieval Clopton Bridge.

Leyland "Titan" PD2/1, 34, (GUE 240), stands in Bridgefoot facing the bridge when about to leave empty on a local service to Justins Avenue, one afternoon in about 1959, just as the local school children start to queue for their bus to take them home. (A.J.Douglas)

16. 30, (JUE 358)

Turning from the bus station into Bridgefoot, 30, (JUE 358), a Leyland-bodied PD2/1, speeds out towards Banbury Road with its conductor standing on the platform.

To the left and behind the bus is Bridge Street. This street led from the crossing point of the River Avon up to the town's medieval centre in High Street, built well above the river's flood plain. Most of Bridge Street was lined by second generation Georgian buildings, with a little Victorian in-filling and was, in this 1963 view, largely unaltered. 1980s redevelopment retained the frontages, but a number of buildings had their innards gutted. (R.F.Mack)

17. 26, (538 EUE)

Leyland "Titan" PD3/4, 26, (538 EUE), starts the climb up Bridge Street away from the Unicorn public house and the row of telephone boxes on the approach to Clopton Bridge. The bus is working on the West Green Drive local town service in 1969 before the road was rebuilt with a central reservation. (F.W.York)

18. 38, (GUE 244)

With a splendid Armstrong-Siddeley "Typhoon" parked nose-in behind it, GUE 244, numbered 38 in the Stratford Blue fleet, waits at the bottom of Bridge Street next to the wrought-iron work of the Mulberry Tree Restaurant. The bus is working on the L4 service to Banbury Road in June 1953 when the Union Jack flags were flying to celebrate the Coronation. At the top of the hill is the octagonal turreted former Market House built in 1821. (A.M.Wright)

19. 29, (JUE 357)

Descending Bridge Street is 29, (JUE 357), a two year old Leyland "Titan" PD2/1 with a Leyland H30/26R body. The Georgian buildings behind the bus lead up the hill to the corner of High Street and the former home of Shakespeare's daughter, Judith Quiney. Like many of the half-timbered buildings in the town, this jettied building dates from immediately after the fires of 1594 and 1595, which destroyed much of the town.

Lands' tobacconist shop has advertisements for the long-forgotten Gold Flake brand of cigarette, while equally long departed cars such as the 1936 Morris Twelve on the left and the leather-covered roofed post-war Riley "Pathfinder" are parked in the street. (R.Marshall)

20. 39, (539 EUE) / 36, (536 EUE)

The original Stratford-upon-Avon Motors route was to Ann Hathaway's Cottage at Shottery. This service was initiated in 1927. About forty-two years later, 39, (539 EUE), a Leyland "Titan" PD3/4, which had sixty-one more seats than the original Chevrolets, is parked in Wood Street before setting out to Shottery. Built in 1963, this bus was by now renumbered 27. Similar vehicle, 36, (536 EUE), renumbered 24, follows on the West Green Drive service. (Bristol Vintage Bus Group)

21. 32, (GUE 238) / 27, (JUE 355)

27, (JUE 355), a 1950 all-Leyland PD2/1, pulls out and overtakes 32, (GUE 238), a similar bus built two years earlier, when working the Redlands and Toll House service. This route was later to become the West Green Drive L2 service. The older bus is on the Shottery service. This bus stop, at the top of Wood Street was outside the half-timbered building, somewhat incongruously occupied by a gas showroom. Today the buildings house a jewellers and a charity shop. (R.F.Mack)

22. 41, (GUE 247)

Leyland "Tiger" PS1, 41, (GUE 247), one of the ten N.C.B.-bodied single-deckers of 1948, passes along Rother Street on the 5 route having come in from Evesham. Parked in front of the Civic Hall are a wonderful selection of cars including a pre-war Standard Flying10 and a Warwickshire registered Morris "Minor" and these date this scene to about 1956. (R.F.Mack)

23. 32, (GUE 238)

In Rother Street in 1957 is 32, (GUE 238), having returned from Shottery. This Leyland PD2/1 of 1948 is parked alongside an unusual Surrey-registered 1930s special. The three-storied building behind Woodward's Fordson E83W van is Stratford's Civic Hall dating from about 1840, while next to it is the pinnacle spire of the Congregational Church built in 1880. (R.F.Mack)

24. 39, (GUE 245)

Beyond Rother Street and the Market Place is Greenhill Street. This led to the former Great Western railway station which is still used today for passenger services along the North Warwickshire line to Birmingham. Beyond the railway station is Alcester Road which had been developed with housing in the 1950s.

39, (GUE 245), still with its blue-painted radiator, is working on the West Green Drive service. The Leyland double-decker is waiting at the traffic lights to turn left into Grove Road on its way to this out-of-town estate. (A.J.Douglas)

25. 4, (671 HNX)

The Stratford town local service served Arden Street where the local hospital was situated. The route went out of Stratford along Birmingham Road until Justins Avenue was reached. This was another council housing estate which Stratford Blue served, in this case with a half hourly service.

Leyland "Titan" PD3A/1, 4, (671 HNX), of 1964, is loading up passengers before returning to the town centre and the Bridge Street terminus. (A.J.Douglas)

PRICE 6d   7th OCTOBER, 1961

UNTIL FURTHER NOTICE

STRATFORD "BLUE"

OFFICIAL TIME TABLE

Subject to Revision at Short Notice

HEAD OFFICE, GARAGE, TRAVEL BUREAU:
WARWICK ROAD
STRATFORD-UPON-AVON
TELEPHONE: STRATFORD 4181

PARCEL ENQUIRY OFFICE:
RED LION 'BUS STATION
STRATFORD-UPON-AVON
TELEPHONE STRATFORD 4181

KINETON GARAGE:
BROOKHAMPTON LANE,
KINETON
TELEPHONE: KINETON 265

STRATFORD " BLUE "—ALWAYS AT YOUR SERVICE

HERALD PRESS, STRATFORD-UPON-AVON

Stratford Blue Garages

Stratford garage

1. 41,(GUE 247) / 54, (JUE 352) / 49, (GUE 255)

The purpose-built garage in Stratford-upon-Avon was situated at the corner of Guild Street and Warwick Road. It had been constructed in 1933 and rebuilt and extended only two years before this photograph was taken.

The main exit was almost opposite the entrance to the Red Lion Bus Station in Warwick Road. In September 1954, a cross-braced mechanic walks back into the garage and passes the Willowbrook-bus bodied Leyland "Tiger" PS2/1, 54, (JUE 352). This would eventually become the only one of the six PS2s not to be rebodied as a double-decker.

On either side of it are Northern Coach Builders bodied Leyland "Tiger" PS1, 41, (GUE 247), to the left and 49, (JUE 255), to the right. (R.Knibbs)

2. 54, (JUE 352) / 36, (GUE 242) and unidentified PS2/3

The depths of Stratford Blue's garage frequently revealed real gems that were normally hidden from the public. While a standard Leyland "Titan" PD2/1, 36, (GUE 242), peaks out of the garage on the left and one of the two Willowbrook bus-bodied Leyland "Tiger" PS2/1s. 54, (JUE 352), is parked in the centre of the Warwick Road exit, the real interest is on the right.

An unidentified PS2/3 is parked, uncommonly, nose into the entrance. It is one of the dual purpose Willowbrook-bodied vehicles. The difference between the bus-bodied PS2/1 and the dual-purpose PS2/3 was that the chassis of the latter had a drop-frame extension. This was to allow coachbuilders to incorporate a luggage boot in the rear of their designs for either a coach or, as in this case, a 'semi-coach'.

This unidentified PS2/3, from this vantage point, reveals its twin rear windows, whereas the PS2/1 versions, (54 and 55), had three windows, with the middle one incorporating the rear emergency exit door. This view also shows the large rear luggage boot which made these dual-purpose vehicles so suitable for long distance coach substitute work. (L.Mason)

3. 19, (2769 NX) / 39, (GUE 245) / 34, (GUE 240) / 58, (3958 UE) /59, (8222NX)

In 1963, most of the buses had changed but the way they were parked remained the same. The buses came into the garage off Guild Street and after being fuelled and watered, were then driven to the Warwick Road gates, which allowed for an easy departure. The driver of 19, (2769 NX) is preparing to leave the garage through this main exit. The two Leyland "Titan" PD2/1s, 39, (GUE 245) on the right and 34, (GUE 240), in the depths of the garage, were in their last year of service. Half-hidden on the left is 58, (3958 UE), the Duple-bodied Ford. On the right, similarly half-hidden, is 59, (8222 NX), the second-hand Bedford SB3, also with a Duple C41F body. This coach had been purchased in 1962 from Warwickshire County Garage and which would, like the PD2/1s, also be withdrawn by the end of 1963. (R.F.Mack)

4. 8 (GUE 2D) /20, (TNX 454)

By 1969, the sign above the garage doors to the Stratford garage had been altered to the new style fleet name. On the 6 August of that year, 8, (GUE 2D), the last of the PD3A/1s and the sole surviving PD2/12, 20, (TNX 454), stood at the entrance. Behind the PD3 is one of the Willowbrook-bodied "Tiger Cubs" of 1959. All of these vehicles would still be in service when Midland Red took over the Stratford Blue operation in January 1971. The garage remained open until July 1990 when Midland Red South closed it. (D.J.Little)

5. 56, (OUE 11)

Parked over the pits in the Stratford garage is 56, (OUE 11). This was one of the pair of Leyland "Royal Tiger" PSU1/16s with Burlingham C37C bodies of 1954. These handsome, heavyweight coaches were in front-line service with Stratford Blue for ten years, having been the first coaches purchased new by the company. Behind it, also over the maintenance pits is one of the JUE-registered all-Leyland PD2/1s of 1950, distinguishable by their sliding ventilators. (R.F.Mack)

6. 56, (AAC 21B)

Parked in a corner! Coaches in bus fleets were obviously less used than their bus equivalents. When not being used on an excursion, an express coach service or a private hire they tended to be parked 'out of the way'. So it is here, with 56, (AAC 21B), one of the 1964 pair of Leyland "Leopard L2Ts with Plaxton C41F bodies sitting on its own at the back of the garage. (R.F.Mack)

7. 49, (GUE 255)

The last of the PS1 Leyland "Tigers", 489, (GUE 255), stands at the back entrance to the Stratford Blue garage yard on 30 April 1950. It is only two years old and had spent these early years sharing its duties with some of the ex-North Western Tilling-Stevens. Next to it is the Willowbrook rebodied Tilling-Stevens, 12, (VT 580). (C.Heaps)

8. 20, (TNX 454) / 33, (GUE 239)

The Guild Street side of the garage in Stratford was used to park vehicles that were either about to enter service for the day or to park buses which were about to return to take up duties. One of the 27' long, Willowbrook-bodied Leyland "Titan" PD2/12s, 20, (TNX 454), waits alongside the garage when still fairly new as it still has all the original livery embellishments, including a silver roof and lining-out bands. One wonders, however if the front tyres were quite legal? (A.J.Douglas)

84

9. 40, (2741 AC),/ 42, (2743 AC),/ 29, (JUE 357)

40, (2741 AC) and 42, (2743 AC), are parked in the side yard off Guild Street when fairly new, about 1961. They are both 1959 Willowbrook-bodied Leyland "Tiger Cub" PSUC1/1s with dual-purpose seats. Alongside is 29, (JUE 357), a Leyland "Titan" PD2/1 with its bonnet open revealing a pristine silver-painted Leyland 0.600 engine, although ironically it appears to have lost its silver-painted roof. (A.J.Douglas)

Kineton garage

10. 48, (GUE 254)

Towards the end of their lives, the N.C.B.-bodied Leyland "Tiger" PS1s were repainted in the simplified livery which not only lacked the lining-out, but also the cream waistrail. 48, (GUE 254), stands on the forecourt of Kineton garage on the occasion of an Omnibus Society visit about 1958.

The garage at Kineton was inherited with the take-over of the Kineton Green Bus Services on 1 January 1937. This garage, ten miles away from Stratford, gave the company another useful operating base in South Warwickshire and was used for garaging vehicles on the services to Banbury and the villages below the escarpment of the Cotswold Hills. (S.N.J.White)

11. 46, (3946 UE)

In later days, Kineton garage was home to many of the "Tiger Cubs" and after 1968, was the usual home for the three "Atlanteans". The garage was fairly new when Kineton Green was taken over as their original one had burnt in the summer of 1934, but had been rebuilt in the 1950s to get it up to the high standard of the main garage in Stratford.

46, (3946 UE), one of the Park Royal DP45F bodied Leyland "Tiger Cub" PSUC1/1s of 1960 is parked almost expectantly on the garage's forecourt in about 1969, waiting for its crew to arrive. (A.E.Hall)

12. 59, (HAC 628D) / 11, (NAC 417F)

59, (HAC 628D), the last L2 Leyland "Leopard to be built, stands at Kineton garage in 1969, with a few of it's skirt panels dented. Behind it, in the garage, is 11, (NAC 417F), the last of the PDR1A/1 "Atlanteans".

Some of Kineton's duties were inexorably involved with the military camps to the south of Kineton and the R.A.F. base at Gaydon, which a few years earlier had been famous for its 'V' Bomber aircraft. 59, is still showing the importance of this traffic even at this late date. (A.E.Hall)

13. 11, (NAC 417F) / 1, (668 HNX)

11, (NAC 417F), the last of the Leyland "Atlantean" PDR1A/1s with decidedly odd proportioned Northern Counties H44/31F bodies of 1967 is parked in Kineton garage along with PD3A/1, 1, (668 HNX), in 1969. Although only a little over a year old, the "Atlantean" still has the look of a factory-finish to its paintwork, suggesting that it has been well looked after and garaged under cover. Unfortunately, the famous Flowers Beers adverts had given way to more mundane and less locally made "tipples"! (A.E.Hall)

'After Life'

1. 33, (GUE 239)/ 32, (GUE 238)

The eight Leyland "Titan" PD2/1s of 1948 remained in service with Stratford Blue intact as a group until 1962 when 35, (GUE 241), became the first of the batch to be taken out of service.

Five buses from the class were sold to Priory Coaches, four of them arriving first in January 1963. Three of them, 33, (GUE 239), 32, (GUE 238) and one of the others, are still recognisably ex-Stratford Blue vehicles, although they have been with Priory Coaches for at least one year. (R.F.Mack)

2. 38, (GUE 244)

Another of the 1948-batch of Leyland-bodied PD2/1s, 38, (GUE 244), is parked in company with another of the batch beneath the railway bridge near the railway station. Both are now owned by Priory Coaches of Leamington Spa. The last of the five PD2/1s to be withdrawn lasted until June 1966. (F.W.York)

3. 40, (GUE 246) / 28, (JUE 356)

The Leyland "Tiger" PS1s were sold at the end of 1959 and the beginning of 1960. 40, (GUE 246), was sold to Porthcawl Omnibus Company. It is seen with the latter operator, keeping company with one of the 1950 batch of Leyland "Titan" PD2/1s. This is 28, (JUE 356), which was one of the first two of the 26 to 31 batch to be withdrawn. It is being prepared for a repaint, although it has been used in service with the chalked destination in the windscreen. (R.H.G.Simpson)

4. 42, (GUE 248)

Most of the PS1s seemed to be sold to the Celtic margins. At least seven of them went to Welsh operators, but 42, (GUE 248), went even further afield.

It is seen in Wick with Dunnets Motors in about 1962. Dunnets are based in the hamlet of Keiss. This is about as far north in mainland Scotland as it is possible to get, lying between Wick and John o'Groats on the main A9 road alongside Sinclair's bay on the North Sea coast. (M.Heard)

5. 46, (GUE 252)

By March 1961, 46, (GUE 252), had been sold to Deiniolen Motors of Bangor. Fully repainted in their smart livery, this Leyland "Tiger" PS1 was used for several years plying between its home town of Bangor and the slate quarrying town of Deiniolen. (R.F.Mack)

6. 27, (JUE 355)

G. & G. Coaches of Leamington Spa purchased JUE 355 from Stratford Blue in January 1964 where it remained in service until September 1967. Ironically, on occasions G. & G. vehicles were hired by Midland Red when Leamington garage was short of crews. G. & G. supplied the buses and the drivers while Midland Red supplied the conductors. The hired buses were used on several routes; here JUE 355 turns into Leamington's bus station when working on the 517 service to Coventry. (F.W.York)

7. 28, (JUE 356)

Leyland "Titan" PD2/1, 28, (JUE 356), built in 1950, is in the yard of Kenfig Motors, Kenfig Hill, having been sold by Stratford Blue in 1964. By now it is carrying a proper destination blind for Trecco Bay, rather than a chalked window!

A slightly older former Southdown Leyland PD2/1, JCD 75 is of the same type as the GUE-registered batch, which arrived with Porthcawl Omnibus in August 1965. (R.F.Mack)

8. 23, (MAC 570)

The MAC-registered Leyland "Titan" PD2/12s lasted with Stratford Blue until September 1965 giving them a service life of thirteen years with their original owners.

23, (MAC 570), the first of the batch, was sold to Whieldon's Green Bus Company of Rugeley and became their fleet number 38. It lasted with them until February 1971. The bus is parked in Cannock Bus Station in about 1968. (G.Holt)

9. 22, (TNX 456)

Obviously happy with their purchase of MAC 570 in 1956, Green Bus bought two more PD2/12s from Stratford Blue two years later in November 1967. 22, (TNX 456), was one of the pair of 1956-built Willowbrook H35/28R bodied buses which found their way to Rugeley. It is parked in Lichfield Bus Station with the rather garish GBC logo as Green Bus number 31. (D.R.Harvey Collection)

10. 40, (2741 AC)

In May and June 1971, all the Willowbrook bodied "Tiger Cubs" were sold to Potteries Motor Traction where that type of Leyland underfloor engined chassis was still in regular service. 40, (2741 AC), is seen at Stafford station in 1971 on a service to Newcastle-under-Lyme.

Despite being painted in full P.M.T. red and white livery and having the fleet number 401, the former Stratford Blue bus's stay in North Staffordshire was disappointingly short as it was withdrawn in December 1972. (A.E.Hall)

11. 42, (2743 AC)

The former Stratford Blue Leyland "Tiger Cub" PSUC1/1, 42, (2743 AC), was sold to Creamline of Tonmawr in December 1972 via Potteries Motor Traction. They also bought 44, (2745 AC), from the same batch. Their constant mesh gearboxes made them non-standard in the Midland Red fleet and as they were only forty-one seaters and this batch of AC-registered buses were twelve years old anyway, they were quickly sold. They remained with Creamline for about six years. (A.E.Hall)

12. 36, (536 EUE)

All of the fifteen Leyland "Titan" PD3s were sold to Isle of Man Road Services. The former Stratford Blue 36, (536 EUE), latterly renumbered 24 in October 1967 was purchased in 1972 and became I.O.M.R.S. 57 as MN 57. In April 1979 it was converted to a rather neat open-topper and ran in this form until it was withdrawn in 1982. It is on Douglas Promenade in National Transport ownership during TT week, decked-out with bunting and appropriately advertising Dunlop tyre. (D.R.Harvey Collection)

13. 39, (539 EUE)

Coming out of Laxey, on the A2 road, with the Laxey goods shed of 1903 in the background, is National Transport's 60, (MN 60). This Northern Counties-bodied Leyland "Titan" PD3/4 is on the way back to Douglas.

This bus had been Stratford Blue's 39, (539 EUE), until 1972. It remained in service on 'The Island' until 1980. (A.J.Douglas)

14. 53, (JUE 351)

Three of the rebodied Leyland "Tiger" PS2/3s were sold to G. & G. Coaches of Leamington in July 1971 after being in store in Evesham garage for most of the time after the take-over by Midland Red.

A slightly down-at-heel former Stratford Blue 53, (JUE 351), latterly numbered 35, stands near the G. & G. garage in Leamington Spa. This sixty-three seater would remain in service with G. & G. Coaches until July 1975, being the first of their PS2/3s to be withdrawn. (D.R.Harvey Collection)

15. 3, (670 HNX)

Swinging around the island at the approach to Douglas Bus Station is Isle of Man National Transport's 63, (MN 63). In its red and white livery, its origin as 670 HNX is well hidden. The bus, a Willowbrook-bodied Leyland "Titan" PD3A/1, was purchased by I.o M.R.S. in September 1972. The fifteen PD3 purchases from Stratford Blue were the first second-hand double-deckers purchased by the company. MN 66 was broken up on the old Jurby airfield near the Point of Ayre in March 1983. (A.E.Hall)

16. 7, (GUE 1D)

The first of the two 1966 deliveries of Leyland"Titan" PD3A/1s, 7, (GUE 1D), became Isle of Man Road Services 70, (MN 2670). After withdrawal it was converted to an exhibition vehicle as a Travelling Art Gallery and it is in this role that it is seen on a typical Manx spring day in May 1987 in Peel. (D.R.Harvey)

17. 59, (HAC 628D)

The 30' long Leyland "Leopard", with a Marshall DP41F body of the attractive curved windscreen B.E.T.-design, went into Midland Red ownership as 2059, but remained at Kineton garage until early 1977. After a brief sojourn at Ludlow, it went into store for about a year. HAC 628D was resurrected, painted in an all-yellow livery and converted to a driver instruction vehicle. When the Midland Red empire was split up in September 1981, it was transferred in the same capacity, to Midland Red West.

It is seen at a bus rally in Cannon Hill Park, Birmingham in the mid-1990s immediately after it was rescued for preservation, but before it was repainted back into its original blue and white livery. (M.V.Squires)

18. 11, (NAC 417F)

The three highbridge Leyland "Atlantean" PDR1/2s of late 1967, were sold off within six months of the Midland Red take-over to City of Oxford Motor Services. They became their 904 to 906. The last of the trio, 11, (NAC 417F), is in Oxford's Cornmarket when working on the 2 route to the Cutteslowe Estate. It is being followed by a 'native' Daimler "Fleetline" CRG6LX, 393, (MJO 393H), with a lower-built, much more attractive-looking N.C.M.E. H43/27D body. The "Atlantean", 906, lasted until September 1979 when it was sold for scrap. (M.Bennett)

19. 36, (XNX 136H)

The last new vehicle to enter service with Stratford Blue was 36, (XNX 136H). This was an Alexander coach-bodied Leyland "Leopard". It became Midland Red's 2036 and was painted in the uninspired all-over livery of National Express.

36, or 2036 as it is here, passes along Hales Street near the Coventry Theatre having recently left Pool Meadow Bus Station on a journey to Llandudno on the North Wales coast. (A.E.Hall)

20. 35, (AUE 313J)

The five Leyland "Panther Cubs" were in store for nine months. Similar vehicles had been purchased by the Northern General Group and so it was perhaps a surprise that they did not snap the five up, although perhaps they knew something which Midland Red management did not! After not being exactly sure about what to do with them, having also had industrial relations problems about operating the buses, Midland Red management must have breathed a sigh of relief when they were last seen driving north on the M6!

35, (AUE 313J), formerly XNX 135H), became Preston Corporation's 234 and lasted until June 1983 - so a service life of twelve years showed perhaps that someone loved them. 35 is seen entering Preston's Bus Station. (A.E.Hall)

21. 37, (537 EUE)

Although not in sequence as regards vehicle order, this is the most appropriate photograph to end this section on the 'After Life' of Stratford Blue buses. Probably the last former Stratford Blue bus to remain in service is this one. Seen on 8 October 1996 in Galway, working on an open-top "Authentic Old Galway Town" sightseeing tour is 37, (537 EUE), a Leyland "Titan" PD3/4 with a Northern Counties H41/32F body which entered service in January 1963. What makes this bus interesting is that it ran for sixteen years and has already lasted longer as an open top vehicle than as a normal double-decker. It was cut down to an open-topper when it was in the Isle of Man fleet as their 58, (MN 58), in August 1979.

After withdrawal in 1982 by Isle of Man National Transport, it has run with three more registrations, Q323 TEP, BSV 982 and since it has been owned by Lally Coach Hire of Galway, as seen here, ZV 1466. Old 37 looks in fine fettle in its thirty-fifth year, even if the brewery advertisement has moved from Stratford to Dublin! (R.Weaver)

Stratford Blue Routes

Stratford Town Services

L1	**BRIDGE STREET** -Manor Road-Knights Lane-Tiddington-**ALLESTON**
L2	**BRIDGE STREET-**Cemetery-SHOTTERY-Clarence Road-Church Lane-Redlands Crescent-**WEST GREEN DRIVE,** (Alcester Road End)
L3	**BRIDGE STREET**-Arden Street-**JUSTINS AVENUE**
L4	**BRIDGE STREET**-Manor Road-**BANBURY ROAD**
—	**BRIDGE STREET-**Clarence Road-Church Lane-Redlands Crescent-**WEST GREEN DRIVE**

Main Road Services

5/5A	**STRATFORD**-Welford-Grafton-Bidford-on-Avon-Salford Priors-Harvington-**EVESHAM**
—	**STRATFORD**-Welford-Long Marston-Pebworth-Honeybourne-Bretforton-**EVESHAM**
10	**STRATFORD**-Bidford-on-Avon-Broom-Wixford-**ALCESTER**
30	**KINETON**-Butlers Marston-Pillerton Hersey-Pillerton Priors-Ettington-Goldicote-**STRATFORD**
31	**KINETON**-Combroke-Moreton Paddox-Moreton Morrell-Ashorne-Newbold Pacey-Wellesbourne-Tiddington-**STRATFORD**
32/32A	**KINETON**-Gaydon-Northend-Marlborough Farm(CAD)-Lighthorne-Bishops Tachbrook-**LEAMINGTONSPA**
33	**KINETON**-Moreton Paddox-Moreton Morrell-Newbold Pacey-Ashorne-Bishops Tachbrook-**LEAMINGTON SPA-(WARWICK)**
34	**KINETON**-Gaydon-Northend-Fenny Compton-Farnborough-Little Bourton-**BANBURY**
34/528	**GAYDON(RAF)**-Marlborough Farm(CAD)-Fenny Compton-Warmington-Banbury(North Bar)**BANBURY**(Railway Station)
35A/35B/35C	**KINETON**-Radway-Edgehill Tower-Ratley-Avon Dassett-Warmington-Shotteswell-Hanwell-**BANBURY**
36	**KINETON**-Radway-Ratley-Edgehill Tower-Horley-Hanwell-**BANBURY**
44/519	**STRATFORD**-Long Compton-Chipping Norton-Woodstock-**OXFORD** (with C.O.M.S.)
64/64A	**EVESHAM**-Sedgeberrow-Beckford-Aston Cross-Bishop Cleeve-**CHELTENHAM SPA**
90A	**STRATFORD**-Snitterfield-Wolverton-Norton Lindsey-Hampton-on-the-Hill-**WARWICK-LEAMINGTON SPA**
150	**STRATFORD**-Wootten Wowen-Henley-in-Arden-Hockley Heath-Shirley-**BIRMINGHAM** (with Midland Red)
—	**STRATFORD**-Preston-on-Stour-Admington-Ilmington-**STRETTON-ON-FOSSE**
—	**STRATFORD**-Snitterfield-Hatton Rock-**HAMPTON LUCY**
—	**STRATFORD**-Loxley-Wellesbourne-**WALTON**
—	**STRATFORD**-Wilmcote-Bearley-Snitterfield-Wolverton-Langley-**CLAVERDON**
—	**STRATFORD-**Billlesley-Wilmcote-Aston Cantlow-Little Alne-Great Alne-Haselor-**ALCESTER**

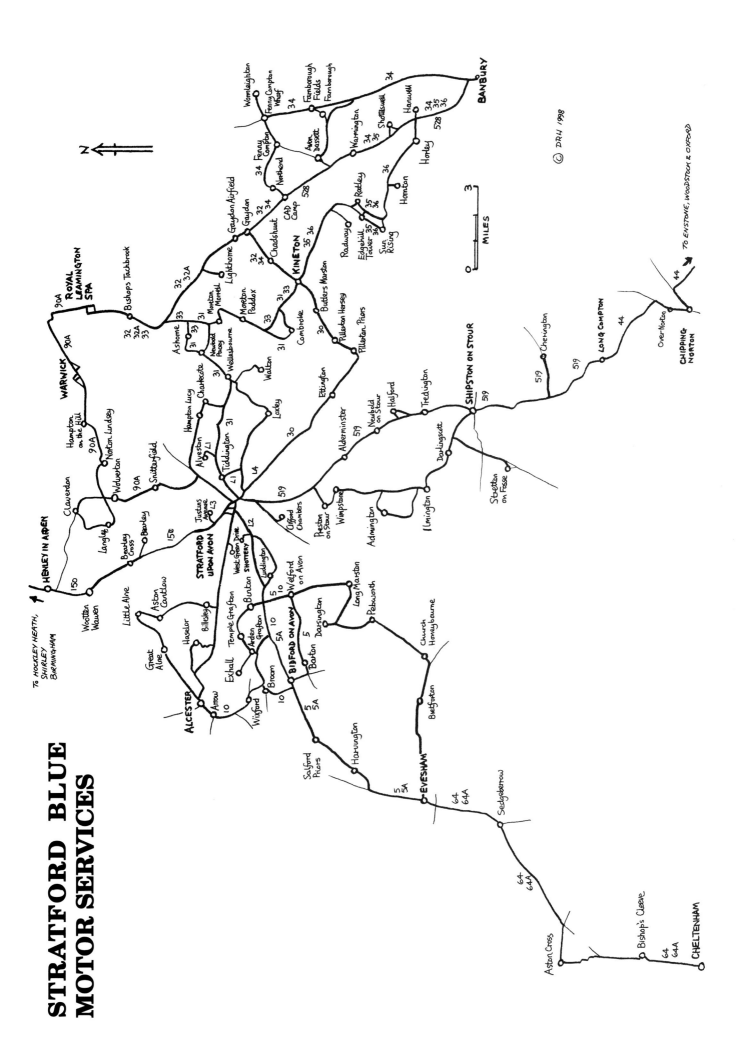

STRATFORD BLUE MOTOR SERVICES

© DRH 1998

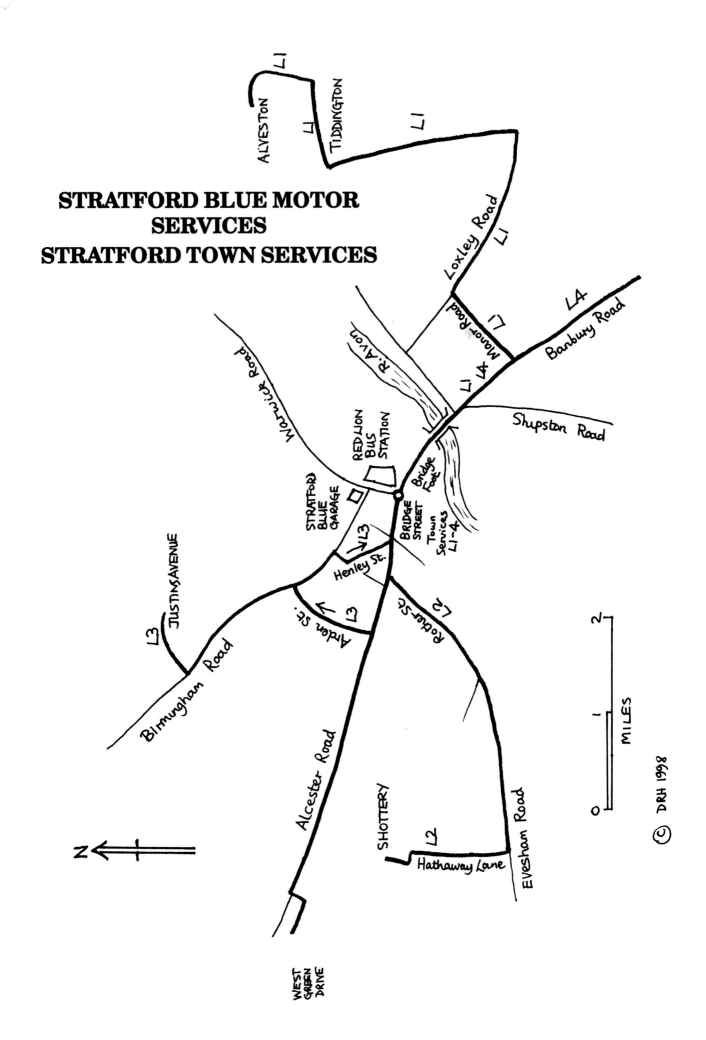

STRATFORD BLUE MOTOR
SERVICES
STRATFORD TOWN SERVICES

Stratford Blue
Destination Blind c.1959

NORTHEND
32A VIA GAYDON
C.A.D.
GAYDON
32 VIA TACHBROOK
KINETON
32A VIA GAYDON
NORTHEND
LEAMINGTON
32 VIA GAYDON
KINETON
30 VIA ETTINGTON
STRATFORD

PRIVATE
SCHOOL
SERVICE
EXTRA
ON HIRE

TIDDINGTON
L1 VIA LOXLEY RD.
ALVESTON
SHOTTERY
L2 FOR ANNE HATHAWAY'S COTTAGE
L3
JUSTINS AVENUE
BRIDGE STREET

BANBURY ROAD
L4 (WATERLOO DRIVE)
L5 VIA SHOTTERY
WEST GREEN DRIVE
L5 VIA ALCESTER RD.

WEST GREEN DRIVE
L6 VIA MASON'S RD.
LONG MARSTON
396 VIA MILCOTE
PEBWORTH
HONEYBOURNE
EVESHAM
396 VIA HONEYBOURNE
STRATFORD
6 VIA WELFORD PEBWORTH
EVESHAM
539 VIA BECKFORD TEDDINGTON HANDS
CHELTENHAM
540 VIA BECKFORD KEMERTON
EVESHAM
5 VIA LUDDINGTON WELFORD
BIDFORD
5A VIA DODWELL GRAFTONS
EXHALL

LUDDINGTON

5 VIA BIDFORD LUDDINGTON
STRATFORD
5A VIA GRAFTONS BIDFORD
EVESHAM
5A VIA MAIN ROAD
SALFORD PRIORS
5A VIA GRAFTONS BIDFORD
BROOM

STRATFORD
44 VIA SHIPSTON CHIPPING NORTON
OXFORD
LONG COMPTON
519 VIA SHIPSTON
480 VIA SHIPSTON
LOWER BRAILES
NEWBOLD
519 VIA ALDERMINSTER
SHIPSTON
8 VIA ADMINGTON ILMINGTON
STRETTON-ON-FOSSE
8 VIA ADMINGTON
ILMINGTON

7 LOXLEY
WELLESBOURNE
9 BEARLEY

11 HAMPTON LUCY
7 WALTON

CLAVERDON
STRATFORD

525 CLIFFORD CHAMBERS
LOWER QUINTON
525 LONG MARSTON
No1 - E.S.D.
CHIPPING CAMPDEN
525 VIA QUINTON
MICKLETON
WARWICK
90A VIA SNITTERFIELD
LEAMINGTON
590 VIA BLACKHILL
STRATFORD
90A VIA NORTON LINDSEY SNITTERFIELD
SNITTERFIELD

STRATFORD
10 VIA BIDFORD WIXFORD
ALCESTER
10 VIA WELFORD IRON CROSS
339 VIA BILLESLEY ASTON CANTLOW
ALCESTER

STRATFORD
150 ON HIRE TO MIDLAND RED
HOCKLEY HEATH
HENLEY-IN-ARDEN
150 ON HIRE TO MIDLAND RED
BIRMINGHAM
159 ON HIRE TO MIDLAND RED
COVENTRY
WARWICK
591 ON HIRE TO MIDLAND RED
COVENTRY
517 ON HIRE TO MIDLAND RED
LEAMINGTON
518 VIA WELLESBOURNE ON HIRE TO MIDLAND RED
STRATFORD

(Courtesy B.W.Ware)

97

Fare Collection And Tickets

Stratford Blue Setright ticket machines

Stratford Blue introduced Setright ticket machines, replacing the old Bell Punch system in 1951. There were several generations of Setright ticket machines. After the company was absorbed into the Birmingham and Midland Motor Omnibus Company on 1 January 1971, within six weeks standard B.M.M.O. decimal machines were introduced.

The company had two garages, the main one in Stratford and Kineton. Unusually, the two garages used different coloured ticket rolls. Kineton always used pink ticket rolls, while Stratford garage had other colours such as khaki, brown, buff and olive green at different times.

Stratford Blue Setright Ticket Machine Numbers

S01-45	1951	Fares ½d - 19/11½d. 1-Jan-Dec.	*Large machine numbers.*
S46-47	9/1956	Fares; (as above)	"
S48-52	1961-62	(As S01-47)	
S1-45	12/1962	**Serial No 50691-50735**	*Small machine numbers.*
S53-54	"	Fares; (as above)	"

Tickets

Printed Information on ticket

Fare	Stage	Date	Serial		Class
SHILLINGS	00-99	DAY	3-FIGURE	Machine	MISC.
PENCE		MONTH		No	SINGLE.
					RETURN.
					WM. D. RTN.
					SCW. RTN.

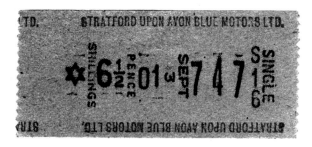

Decimalisation

Some, possibly all, machines converted with decimalisation kits in 1970.

Disposals

It is believed that no machines saw subsequent use after withdrawal.

Stratford-Upon-Avon Blue Motor Services Fleet List

Stratford-upon-Avon Motors Ltd, (S.H.Joiner & G.H.Grail)

Fleet No	Registration No	Chassis		Chassis No	Body	Seating	New	Withdrawn
1	UE 3403	Chevrolet	LM	15374	Allen	B14F	1927	1931
2	UE 3897	"	"	16125	"	"	"	"
3	UE 4189	"	"	?	"	"	"	"
4	UE 4664	"	"	17202	"	"	"	"
5	UE 4665	"	"	17203	"	"	"	"
6	UE 4933	"	"	17635	"	"	"	"
7	UE 4934	"	"	?	"	"	"	"
8	UE 5283	Thornycroft	A2	15353	Hall Lewis	B20F	1928	1936
9	UE 5749	"	"	15336	"	"	"	"
10	UE 6494	"	"	14721	"	"	"	—
11	UE 6734	"	"	14722	"	"	"	—
12	TX 1498	"	A1	12817(1928)	N.C.M.E	"(1929)	1929	1936
13	UT 411	"	"	12846	Hall Lewis	"	"	—
Ex-Wheeler, Kirby Muxloe, 1929								
14	NR 9527	"	"	12804	?	"	"	1933
Ex-Wheeler, Kirby Muxloe, 1929								
15	TX 598	"	"	12769	Hall Lewis	"	"	"
Ex-Barry Associated Motorways, 1929								
16	TX 647	"	"	12767	"	"	"	"
Ex-Barry Associated Motorways, 1929								
17	DF 4771	"	A2	14674	?	"	1928	1936
Ex-Martin, Cheltenham, 1930								
18	TR 1886	"	A1	12778	Hall Lewis	"	"	—
Ex-Martin, Cheltenham, 1930								
—	HO 6332	Thornycroft	BT	10328	?	B26F	1924	1931
Ex-Martin, Cheltenham, 1930								
20	DG 127	Ford	AA	3012506	?	B14	1928	"
Ex-Martin, Cheltenham, 1930								
—	RU 1931	?		?	?	?	?	"
Ex-Martin, Cheltenham, 1930								
—	DF 2319	Graham-Dodge	A	584567	?	B14	?	"
Ex-Martin, Cheltenham, 1930								
—	DF 3696	"		825237	?	B14	1927	"
Ex-Martin, Cheltenham, 1930								

Stratford-upon-Avon Blue Motors, (Balfour Beatty)
Ex-Midland General, Langley Mill

Fleet No	Registration No	Chassis		Chassis No	Body	Seating	New	Withdrawn
19	RA 3869	Tilling-Stevens	B9B	5514	Brush	B30F	1927	1936
Ex- Midland General 39, 1931								
20	RA 3538	"	B10B	5154	"	"	"	1933
Ex-Midland General 27, 1931								

Fleet No	Registration No	Chassis		Chassis No	Body	Seating	New layout	Withdrawn
21	RA 3870	"	B9B	5197	"	"	"	1937
Ex-Midland General 40, 1931								
22	RA 3959	"	B9B	5513	"	"	"	1936
Ex-Midland General 42, 1931								
24	RA 3958	"	B9B	5512	Strachan & Brown	B30F	"	1937
Ex-Midland General 41, 1931								

Ex-Reliance, Bidford-on-Avon

Fleet No	Registration No	Chassis		Chassis No	Body	Seating	New layout	Withdrawn
7	UE 6467	Star	VB4	C810	Willowbrook	B20F	1928	1935
Ex-Reliance, Bidford-on-Avon, 1932								
18	UE 7973	"	"	C887	"	C23F	1929	1936
Ex-Reliance, Bidford-on-Avon, 1932								
—	UE 9816	Guy	OND	9424	Guy	B20F	1930	1932
Ex-Reliance, Bidford-on-Avon, 1932								
—	UE 9319	Guy	OND	9388	Guy	B20F	1929	"
Ex-Reliance, Bidford-on-Avon, 1932								
—	UE 4601	Chevrolet	LM	17487	?	B14F	1927	1930
Reliance, Bidford-on-Avon. Sold 1930								
—	UE 4618	Chevrolet	LM	17010	?	B14F	"	"
Reliance, Bidford-on-Avon. Sold 1930								
—	UE 5447	Chevrolet	LM	18914	?	B14F	"	"
Reliance, Bidford-on-Avon. Sold 1930								
—	WD 1171	Ford	AA	3458762	?	B14F	1930	"
Reliance, Bidford-on-Avon. Sold 1930								
(22)	WD 3338	Albion "Valiant"	PV70	11501E	Harrington	B32F	1932	
Albion Mts, Scotstoun, demonstrator, 1932								
(23)	AMD 739	A.E.C."Regal"	662	6621487	"	C—	1933	1933
A.E.C., Southall, demonstrator, 1933								
20	FG 5227	Commer	4PF	16006	Hall Lewis	B32F	1929	1935
Ex- ? , Fife, via Midland General 1/1933								

Ex-Cheltenham District, Cheltenham

Fleet No	Registration No	Chassis		Chassis No	Body	Seating	New layout	Withdrawn
14	DG 1312	Guy	C	C23679	Guy	B28F	1930	1937
Ex-Cheltenham District Traction 19, 1934								
15	DG 1317	Guy	C	C23684	Guy	B28F	1930	"
Ex-Cheltenham District Traction 24, 1934								
16	DG 1316	Guy	C	C23683	Guy	B28F	1930	"
Ex-Cheltenham District Traction 23, 1934								
20	DG 1310	Guy	C	C23677	Guy	B28F	1930	1937
Ex-Cheltenham District Traction 17, 1934								

Stratford-on-Avon Blue Motor Services (B.M.M.O.)

Fleet No	Registration No	Chassis		Chassis No	Body	Seating	New layout	Withdrawn
17	WK 9631	Maudslay	ML	4518	?	B32F	1929	1937
Ex-Red House Garage, Coventry, 1936								
18	VC 7801	Maudslay	ML	5651	?	B32F	1931	"
Ex-Red House Garage, Coventry, 1936								
23	WK 9708	Maudslay	ML	4481	?	B32F	1929	"
Ex-Red House Garage, Coventry, 1936								
11	VT 34	Tilling-Stevens	B10A2	5134	Willowbrook	B32F	1927	1949
Ex-Kingfisher, Derby and Trent M.T, 1936								
12	VT 580	Tilling-Stevens	B10A2	5547	Willowbrook	B32F	1927	1950
Ex-Kingfisher, Derby and Trent M.T, 1936								

Ex-North Western Road Car Co Ltd, Stockport

Fleet No	Registration No	Chassis		Chassis No	Body	Seating	New layout	Withdrawn
1	DB 5141	Tilling-Stevens	B10A2	5623	Brush	B36R	1928	1939
Ex-N.W.R.C. 241, 10/1936								
2	DB 5152	"	"	5672	Tilling	B32R	"	"
Ex-N.W.R.C. 252, 10/1936								
3	DB 5153	"	"	5673	"	"	"	"
Ex-N.W.R.C. 253, 10/1936								

FleetNo	RegistrationNo	Chassis		Chassis No	Body	Seating layout	New	Withdrawn
4	DB 5154	"	"	5674	"	"	"	"
Ex-N.W.R.C. 254, 10/1936								
5	DB 5184	"	"	5780	"	B36R	"	"
(later 22)Ex-N.W.R.C. 284, 10/1936								
6	DB 5162	Tilling-Stevens	B10A2	5682	Brush	B32R	1928	1939
Ex-N.W.R.C. 262, 10/1936								
7	DB 5157	"	"	5677	Tilling	B32R	"	"
Ex-N.W.R.C. 257, 10/1936								
8	DB 5158	"	"	5678	"	"	"	"
Ex-N.W.R.C. 258, 10/1936								
9	DB 5159	"	"	5679	Brush	B32R	"	"
Ex-N.W.R.C. 259, 10/1936								
10	DB 5140	"	"	5622	"	"	"	"
Ex-N.W.R.C. 240, 10/1936								
14	DB 5147	"	"	5667	Tilling	B32R	"	"
Ex-N.W.R.C. 247, 10/1936								
15	DB 5130	"	"	5612	Brush	B36R	"	"
Ex-N.W.R.C. 230, 10/1936								
16	DB 5156	"	"	5676	Tilling	B32R	"	"
Ex-N.W.R.C. 256, 1/1937								
17	DB 5177	"	"	5773	"	B36R	"	"
Ex-N.W.R.C. 277, 1/1937								
18	DB 5155	"	"	5675	"	B32R	"	"
Ex-N.W.R.C. 255, 1/1937								
19	DB 5163	"	"	5683	Brush	"	"	"
Ex-N.W.R.C. 263, 1/1937								
20	DB 5190	"	"	5786	Tilling	B36R	"	"
Ex-N.W.R.C. 290, 1/1937								
21	DB 5166	"	"	5686	Brush	B32R	"	"
Ex-N.W.R.C. 166, 1/1937To tree-lopper 1/1944-1/1952								

Kineton Green Bus Co, Kineton 1/1937, but not operated

FleetNo	RegistrationNo	Chassis		Chassis No	Body	Seating layout	New	Withdrawn
—	UE 4971	Chevrolet	LM	?	?	B14F	1927	?
—	UE 6108	Chevrolet	LM	?	?	"	1928	?
—	UE 6792	Reo	FAX	4265	?	B20F	1928	1934
—	UE 7917	"	C	25522	?	"	1929	"
—	UE 8132	Chevrolet	LQ	50201	?	B14F	"	?
—	UE 9167	Reo	GE	93	?	B26F	"	1934
—	WO 1057	B.A.T.		172	?	C20F	1927	1934
—	UO 7471	Leyland "Lion"	PLSC3	46749	Hall Lewis	B32D	1928	1937
Ex-Devon General 117, 1934								
—	UO 7851	Leyland "Lioness"	PLC1	47423	Hall Lewis	C26D	"	"
Ex-Devon General 118, 1934								
—	UO 7852	Leyland "Lioness"	PLC1	47424	"	"	"	"
Ex-Devon General 119, 1934								
—	UO 9690	Leyland "Lion"	PLSC3	47514	Hall Lewis	B32D	1929	"
Ex-Devon General 124, 1934								

Ex-Leamington & Warwick, Royal Leamington Spa

FleetNo	RegistrationNo	Chassis		Chassis No	Body	Seating layout	New	Withdrawn
23	UE 9323	Daimler	CF6	7322	Brush	B32F	1929	1938
Ex-Leamington & Warwick, 9, 10/1937								
—	UE 9916	"	"	7336	"	"	1930	1937
Ex-Leamington & Warwick, 20, on hire 1937								

Ex-West Yorkshire Road Car Co. Ltd, Harrogate

FleetNo	RegistrationNo	Chassis		Chassis No	Body	Seating layout	New	Withdrawn
1	WX 2121	Tilling-Stevens	B10A2	6709	Tilling	B32F	3/1930	8/1948
Ex-West Yorkshire R.C. 265, 10/1938								
2	WX 2131	"	"	6719	United	"	"	3/1948
Ex-West Yorkshire R.C. 275, 10/1938								

Fleet No	Registration No	Chassis		Chassis No	Body	Seating layout	New	Withdrawn
3	WX 2126	"	"	6714	"	"	"	11/1948
		Ex-West Yorkshire R.C. 270, 10/1938						
4	WX 2134	"	"	6722	"	"	4/1930	12/1948
		Ex-West Yorkshire R.C. 278, 10/1938						
5	WX 2120	Tilling-Stevens	B10A2	6708	Tilling	"	3/1930	2/1949
		Ex-West Yorkshire R.C. 264, 10/1938						
6	WX 2152	"	"	6740	"	"	4/1930	3/1947
		Ex-West Yorkshire R.C. 296, 10/1938						
7	WX 2151	"	"	6739	"	"	"	12/1946
		Ex-West Yorkshire R.C. 295, 10/1938						
8	WX 2148	"	"	6736	United	"	"	10/1946
		Ex-West Yorkshire R.C. 292, 10/1938						
9	WX 2125	"	"	6713	Tilling	"	"	11/1948
		Ex-West Yorkshire R.C. 269, 10/1938						
10	WX 2130	"	"	6718	United	"	3/1930	5/1948
		Ex-West Yorkshire R.C. 274, 10/1938						
14	WX 2118	"	"	6706	"	"	2/1930	12/1948
		Ex-West Yorkshire R.C. 262, 10/1938						
15	WX 2133	"	"	6721	"	"	4/1930	5/1948
		Ex-West Yorkshire R.C. 277, 10/1938						
16	WX 2144	"	"	6732	Tilling	"	"	11/1948
		Ex-West Yorkshire R.C. 288, 10/1938						
17	WX 2141	"	"	6729	Roe	"	"	"
		Ex-West Yorkshire R.C. 285, 10/1938						
18	WX 2153	"	"	6741	"	"	5/1930	10/1948
		Ex-West Yorkshire R.C. 297, 10/1938						
19	WX 2150	"	"	6738	"	"	4/1930	12/1948
		Ex-West Yorkshire R.C. 294, 10/1938						
20	WP 8277	Maudslay	ML3	5189	W.D.Smith	C32R	1934	1946
		Ex-P.Owen, Abberley, 1938						
21	WP 3425	"	"	5082	"	"	1933	1946
		Ex-P.Owen, Abberley, 1938						
22	JO 2354	A.E.C. "Regent"	661	6611129	Park Royal	L24/24R	1931	3/1948
		Ex-City of Oxford M.S. G167, 3/1940						
23	HA 4942	S.O.S."M"		1093	Ransomes S & J	B34F	1929	1948
		Ex-B.M.M.O. A1032, 1944						
(26)	AHA 619	S.O.S. "OLR"		2037	Short	B34F	1935	1948
		On loan ex-B.M.M.O., 1675, 1945-1948						
(24)	JA 6972	Leyland "Tiger"	TS7	9493	Harrington	C32F	1936	1950
		On loan ex-Majestic Express, Stockport 1945-1950						
(25)	JA 6973	"	"	9494	"	"	"	"
		On loan ex-Majestic Express, Stockport 1945-1950						

Ex-North Western Road Car Co Ltd, Stockport

Fleet No	Registration No	Chassis		Chassis No	Body	Seating layout	New	Withdrawn
20	DB 9375	Tilling-Stevens	B10A2	6764	E.C.O.C. (1935)	B31R	1930	1950
		Ex-N.W.R.C. 475, 1946						
21	DB 9377	"	"	6766	"	"	"	"
		Ex-N.W.R.C. 477, 1946						
26	DB 9395	"	"	6784	"	"	"	"
		Ex-N.W.R.C. 495, 1946						
27	DB 9368	"	"	6757	"	"	"	"
		Ex-N.W.R.C. 468, 1946						
28	DB 9362	"	"	6583	"	"	"	"
		Ex-N.W.R.C. 462, 1946						
29	DB 9380	"	"	6769	"	"	"	"
		Ex-N.W.R.C. 480, 1946 Became tree-cutter TC1, 1/1952-1/1955						
30	DB 9389	"	"	6778	"	"	"	"
		Ex-N.W.R.C. 489, 1946						

Fleet No	Registration No	Chassis		Chassis No	Body	Seating layout	New	Withdrawn
31	DB 9397	"	"	6756	"	"	"	"
Ex-N.W.R.C. 497, 1946								
32	GUE 238	Leyland "Titan"	PD2/1	481040	Leyland	H30/26R	3/1948	1/1963
33	GUE 239	"	"	481038	"	"	"	"
34	GUE 240	"	"	481039	"	"	"	4/1963
35	GUE 241	"	"	480945	"	"	"	1/1963
36	GUE 242	"	"	481042	"	"	"	"
37	GUE 243	"	"	480944	"	"	"	"
38	GUE 244	"	"	481043	"	"	"	"
39	GUE 245	"	"	481041	"	"	"	"
40	GUE 246	Leyland "Tiger"	PS1	483184	N.C.B.	B34F	11/1948	3/1960
41	GUE 247	"	"	483185	"	"	12/1948	"
42	GUE 248	"	"	483268	"	"	"	"
43	GUE 249	"	"	483341	"	"	9/1948	"
44	GUE 250	"	"	483445	"	"	11/1948	"
45	GUE 251	"	"	480757	"	"	1/1949	11/1960
46	GUE 252	"	"	480758	"	"	"	"
47	GUE 253	"	"	480759	"	"	"	"
48	GUE 254	"	"	480760	"	"	"	"
49	GUE 255	"	"	480761	"	"	"	"
50	JUE 348	Leyland "Tiger"	PS2/3	495826	Willowbrook	DP34F 50763	3/1950	9/1971
Renumbered 32				*495826Yrebodied N.C.M.E. H35/28F, 5840 (1963)*				
51	JUE 349	"	"	495827	"	50764	4/1950	"
Renumbered 33				*495827Yrebodied N.C.M.E. H35/28F, 5839 (1963)*				
52	JUE 350	"	"	495828	"	50765	"	"
Renumbered 34				*495828Yrebodied N.C.M.E. H35/28F, 5838 (1963)*				
53	JUE 351	"	"	495829	"	50766	"	"
Renumbered 35				*495829Yrebodied N.C.M.E. H35/28F, 5841 (1963)*				
54	JUE 352	"	PS2/1	495824	"	B34F 50770	"	1963
55	JUE 353	"	"	495825	"	" 50769	"	1970
Renumbered 16 (later 31)				*495825Yrebodied Roe H35/28F GO5336 (8/1961)*				
26	JUE 354	Leyland "Titan" PD2/1		502520	Leyland	H30/26R	8/1950	1/1964
27	JUE 355	"	"	502521	"	"	"	"
28	JUE 356	"	"	502519	"	"	"	"
29	JUE 357	"	"	502566	"	"	"	"
30	JUE 358	"	"	502565	"	"	"	"
31	JUE 359	"	"	502567	"	"	"	"
23	MAC 570	Leyland "Titan" PD2/12		521067	Leyland	H32/26RD	5/1952	9/1965
24	MAC 571	"	"	521521	"	"	"	"
25	MAC 572	"	"	521522	"	"	"	"
56	OUE 11	Leyland "Royal Tiger" PSU1/16		532684	Burlingham	C37C 5110	4/1954	1/1964
57	OUE 12	"	"	532683	"	5109	"	"
TC1	DHA 731	S.O.S.	SON	2542	ex-B.M.M.O2113	1938	tree-cutter	1/1955-1962
20	TNX 454	Leyland "Titan"	PD2/12	556415	Willowbrook	H35/28RD 56710	3/1956	4/1971
21	TNX 455	"	"	556416	"	56711	"	10/1967
22	TNX 456	"	"	556413	"	56712	"	"
40	2741 AC	Leyland "Tiger Cub" PSUC1/1		587177	Willowbrook	DP41F 59287	1959	5/1971
41	2742 AC	"	"	587178	"	59285	"	"
42	2743 AC	"	"	587190	"	59284	"	"
43	2744 AC	"	"	587191	"	59286	"	"
44	2745 AC	"	"	587113	"	B45F 59288	"	"
—	SHA 446	Leyland "Titan"	PD2/12	530093	Leyland	H30/26RD	1953	—
On loan ex-B.M.M.O. 4046, 12/1959-12/1959								

Fleet No	Registration No	Chassis		Chassis No	Body	Seating layout	New	Withdrawn
—	398 JTB	Leyland "Atlantean" PDR1/1		582861	M.C.W.	H44/34F	1958	—
Leyland Motors demonstrator 2/1960-2/1960								
17	2767 NX	Leyland "Titan"	PD3/4	592208	Willowbrook	H41/32F 59441	2/1960	8/1971
18	2768 NX	"	"	592229	"	"59442	3/1960	"
19	2769 NX	"	"	592230	"	"59443	"	"
58	3958 UE	Ford Thames	570E	52985	Duple	C41F	1961	—

Ex-Hayward & Ball, Warwickshire County Garage, Stratford, 3/1962

Fleet No	Registration No	Chassis		Chassis No	Body	Seating layout	New	Withdrawn
59	8222NX	Bedford	SB3	80334	Duple	C41F	1960	1965
—	LNX 488	"	SB	2374	?	C35F	8/1951	1962
—	LWD 567	"	SB	?	?	C33F	1952	"
45	3945 UE	Leyland "Tiger Cub"PSUC1/1		606329	Park Royal	B45F 45196	11/1960	4/1971
46	3946 UE	"	"	606330	"	45197	"	"
47	3947 UE	"	"	606365	"	45198	"	"
48	3948 UE	"	"	606366	"	45199	"	"
49	5449 WD	Leyland "Tiger Cub"PSUC1/1		617455	Marshall	B45FB3027	2/1962	4/1971
50	5450 WD	"	"	617540	"	B3028	"	"
51	5451 WD	"	"	617468	"	B3029	"	"
52	5452 WD	"	"	617469	"	B3030	"	"
53	5455 WD	"	"	617541	"	DP41F B3031	"	"
Originally numbered 55								
36	536 EUE	Leyland "Titan"	PD3/4	623278	N.C.M.E.	H41/32F5843	1/1963	11/1971
37	537 EUE	"	"	623279	"	5842	"	"
38	538 EUE	"	"	623593	"	5845	"	"
39	539 EUE	"	"	623594	"	5844	"	"
54	CWD 33C	Leyland "Leopard" PSU3/3R	L21695		Weymann	B53F M1660	1965	5/1976
Originally numbered 60								
55	436 GAC	"	"	L00178	Duple (N)	C49F 137/7	6/1963	11/1972
56	AAC 21B	"	L2T	L04272	Plaxton C41F	642978	5/1964	1/1976
57	AAC 22B	"	"	L04273	"	642979	"	"
58	DAC 753C	"	PSU3/3R	L4035	Duple (N) C49F	163/58	6/1965	"
Originally numbered 61								
59	HAC 628D	"	L2	L60880	Marshall	DP41F B3651	1966	5/1978
1	668 HNX	Leyland "Titan"	PD3A/1	L02477	Willowbrook H41/32FCF682		12/1963	12/1971
2	669 HNX	"	"	L02478	"	CF683	"	"
3	670 HNX	"	"	L02479	"	CF684	1/1964	5/1972
4	671 HNX	"	"	L02480	"	CF685	"	"
5	672 HNX	"	"	L02481	"	CF686	"	"
6	673 HNX	"	"	L02482	"	CF687	"	"
7	GUE 1D	Leyland "Titan"	PD3A/1	L43176	WillowbrookH41/32F CF 1152		1/1966	6/1972
8	GUE 2D	"	"	L43177	"	CF 1153	"	7/1972
—	THA 146	B.M.M.O.	D7	4146	M.C.C.W.	H32/26R	1954	
On loan ex- B.M.M.O. 4146, 11/1967-12/1967								
—	767 BHA	"	"	4767	"	H37/26R	1957	
On loan ex-B.M.M.O. 4767, 11/1967-12/1967								
9	NAC 415F	Leyland "Atlantean"PDR1A/1		700022	N.C.M.E.	H44/31F 6559	12/ 1967	5/1971
10	NAC 416F	"	"	700023	"	6557	"	"
11	NAC 417F	"	"	700045	"	6558	"	"
36	XNH 136H	Leyland "Leopard"PSU3A/4R	7001612		AlexanderDP49F 135/Y/2869/1		1970	12/1982
31	AUE 309J	Leyland "Panther"PSUR1A/1		902361	Marshall B41D	B4441	10/1970	7/1971
32	AUE 310J	"	"	902362	"	B4442	"	"
33	AUE 311J	"	"	902363	"	B4444	"	"
34	AUE 312J	"	"	902364	"	B4443	"	"
35	AUE 313J	"	"	902365	"	B4445	"	"